THE *Cook*

The
COOK

Harry Kressing [pseud.]

Random House New York

Cop. 2

1065691

TO

M. E. G.

Man is a cooking animal
—OLD COOK BOOK

Man is a dining animal
—OLD COOK BOOK

I

I

One hill stood out. It was steeper than the others, and higher. Also, it had no peak. While the rounded, wooded tops of the surrounding hills undulated, one into the other, this one broke the rhythm with an abrupt, flat surface.

For a few minutes Conrad just stared, shielding his eyes from the sun. Then he dismounted and dragged his bicycle off the road. When he was out of sight he chained it to a tree and concealed his rucksack under some brush. Then he started up the hill.

It was an easy climb until near the top. There he discovered a sheer cliff. It was at least twenty feet high. But if it ran all the way around no one would be able to reach the plateau.

Nevertheless, he circumambulated rather more than half the hill without finding a break in the cliff face. He began to have doubts. Possibly ladders were required. They could be brought, or lowered down.

Disappointed, he increased his pace.

In his haste he nearly missed the stairway cut in the cliff face. The steps were very narrow and high, and at a nasty angle.

When he gained the plateau he encountered another barrier: a deep moat, with water in the bottom and smooth, sheer sides, encircled the fantastic castle-like structure. There was a single drawbridge, up and locked. There was absolutely no way to get across.

After circling the moat several times he sat down and looked at the castle. It was essentially Gothic, constructed of blue-gray stone, rising in hexagonal design some four stories from the ground. It was very big, about two hundred rooms. It was also in an excellent state of upkeep.

The grounds were also beautifully kept.

"Why then," he asked himself, "do I have a feeling no one lives up here? And if no one lives up here, why is it all kept up so?"

Several miles in the distance a small town, spired and pastel-shaded, nestled in a wooded valley.

"That must be Cobb," Conrad thought.

He would ask someone in Cobb about the castle.

❧

". . . only the gardeners and the maintenance people go up to the Prominence now. And some architects from the City. But that's all. The Hills and the Vales never go. Of course, the Hills still own all the hill land, the lumber and the quarries, and the Vales have all the lowland with the lakes and the town. That's how they got their names—but I guess I told you that before. And the road still divides their property, the one you came on from the City."

For the price of a few beers the story of the castle was Conrad's.

The castle was known as the Prominence.

The tavern-keeper rambled in the telling and repeated himself. But he seemed to know what he was talking about. He did not contradict himself.

The Prominence was the ancestral home of the Cobb family for generations. It had been conceived by the first Cobb—A. Cobb—who also founded the town and for whom it was named.

The descendants of A. Cobb prospered, and within a few generations gained control of practically all the good hill land and all the good lowland.

They became, of course, the one great landowning family in the area.

Subsequent descendants consolidated and extended the family holdings.

The hill land and the lowland were administered as two separate estates. By what amounted to a hereditary stewardship, the hill estate was worked and managed by the Hill clan, and the lowland by the Vale clan. The two clans hated each other.

This system continued until no more male heirs were born to the Cobb family. There were then only two Cobb daughters. One was in love with the chief of the Hill clan, and the other with the chief of the Vale clan.

Old man Cobb was unable to stop his daughters from marrying these men. He also failed to effect a rapprochement between the two clans. And thus his will:

The hill land to one daughter and heirs, the lowland to the other. Both estates entailed against gift or sale, and an equal charge laid upon them for the upkeep of the Prominence, which

was to remain unoccupied until the two estates were reunited
by marriage. The entail was to be renewed as successive heirs
came of age, failing which the two estates were to be apportioned
among certain charitable institutions in the City.

The entail had been duly renewed by successive generations
of Hills and Vales and the will of old Cobb was still in force.

A few years back it was thought there would be a Hill-Vale
marriage and that at last the Cobb descendants could resume
their proper residence.

"The Hills and the Vales no longer feud," explained the tavern-
keeper. "They're on the best of terms. They have separate
residences, but they're always visiting and eating together. If
there's any competition between them it's over who lays the
best table, or who has the best cook.

"The Vale name is about to die out. There are only three
Vales left: Mr. and Mrs. and their daughter Daphne. Mr. and
Mrs. Vale are in middle years and in poor health."

There were four Hills: Mr. and Mrs.; a son, Harold; and
a daughter, Ester—twins. The elder Hills were large and
robust, in excellent health. The twins had the Hill frame, the
Hill health and the Hill good looks.

The Hill twins were in their twenties, a year or two older
than Daphne Vale.

For years Daphne and the twins were inseparable, and it
had always been assumed that she and Harold would marry
in due course.

And then Daphne started getting fat. And she got fatter and
fatter—"just everything she ate turned to fat. That's what the
doctor said. And he said there wasn't a thing he could do about
it.

"And now she's as fat as a pig, although no one ever sees her
except the servants and the Hills, because she never goes any
place. She's probably ashamed of herself. And of course no one
could expect Harold to marry her now."

II

Conrad asked the tavern-keeper how he could get to the Hill mansion and was told that it was on the side of a hill about a mile and a half from town.

He had about an hour before his appointment and he decided to look the town over.

The townspeople also got a good chance to look him over.

He is very eye-catching as he wheels his bicycle beside him, a rucksack strapped on its fender.

He is at least six feet six inches tall—a good head taller than anyone else on the street—and extremely thin, to the point of cadaverousness. His features are hawk-like, with a veritable beak of a nose. From sunken eye sockets, large coal-black eyes look out sharply. Black hair curls from beneath his hat down his neck to the collar.

He is dressed all in black. His trousers are wrapped tight around his ankles inside long black socks.

Indeed, he looks "just like a hungry black eagle," as one of the shopkeepers described him later that day in a tavern, and all who had seen Conrad nodded.

The small town of Cobb seemed prosperous enough. Its streets were cobblestone. They were clean and in a decent state of repair.

There was one main street, and several cross-streets.

The buildings were constructed of wood and stone—doubtless from the Hill woodland and stone quarries.

As for the stores—to one accustomed to the City, Cobb was a keen disappointment.

There were three butcher shops. Conrad went into each one and examined the meat critically. None of it met with his approval. Either it was poor meat to begin with or it had not been cut with any professional competence, and he told each butcher this in no uncertain terms, raising his voice so that the other customers in the shop should know what he thought. In one shop he even accused the butcher of lying—the man was trying to sell as a leg of lamb what was obviously a worn-out leg of mutton. The man denied this, but Conrad replied that the old leg wouldn't get tender in a forge, and as the customers stared at him agape, he threw it on the floor and walked out.

He went into the two fish markets, and complained that the fish was not fresh and that the choice was too limited.

There were five greengroceries. He only went into two of them—the others obviously catered to poor people—and in both he told the proprietors their fruit and vegetables weren't fit for human consumption.

And in the shop of a provisioner of canned goods: "Is this all you have?"

The old storekeeper plucked at his beard. "You want to order a large quantity of something?"

"Don't be obtuse," Conrad snapped. "I'm referring to your selection. Look at it—what can be gotten fresh in Cobb, or in a living or raw state, or dried or salted, you have in cans. And what can't be so gotten you don't have at all. In brief, your shop serves no purpose. —But we'll change that, mark my word."

Besides the food stores, there were a glassware and china shop, a small bookstall, and a hardware store. At each one of these he made inquiries, just as in the other places.

He even went into Cobb's premier dining establishment, the Prominence Inn, and asked to see the day's menu. As he scanned it he got a chance to look at two or three of the dishes being served. Returning the menu to the head waiter he informed him icily that when he, Conrad, should decide to eat there he would first inspect the kitchen—which was doubtless filthy—and then he would personally supervise the preparation . . .

After he had completed his survey of the facilities in Cobb, it was time to start for the Hill mansion. He found the way easily enough.

Because of the high trees on both sides, the road was already partly hidden in shadows, though it was only late afternoon.

Making his way up the hill, Conrad recalled with satisfaction the scene in the butcher shop: how everyone had stared at him and listened to what he said about the old leg of mutton, and how they had seen him throw it into the blood-splattered sawdust.

The word would also spread about what had happened in the hardware store. It was probably already spreading as the people began dropping into the taverns for their evening drink.

Conrad's thin and hard lips curled in what might have been a smile.

He had gone into the hardware store to examine the cutlery. The proprietor hovered, trying to make a sale.

"Let me see your best chef's knife," Conrad said, "the one that holds the keenest edge."

The man proudly drew from the case a gleaming knife.

"Is that the best you have?" Conrad asked.

"I have no doubt but that it's the best in Cobb," answered the proprietor, holding out the knife. But Conrad disdained it, and from somewhere in his clothing produced a truly wicked-looking blade.

"Here," he said; "cut the two blades together and then we'll see whether that's the best knife in Cobb."

The proprietor hesitated, but the other customers had heard Conrad's challenge, and gathered around.

Giving his own knife the better angle, the storekeeper cut the blades one against the other. Nothing happened.

"You must be weak," Conrad said, and taking the knives from the man's hands, cut the blades at an equal angle—slicing off in one long metal sliver the entire cutting edge of the proprietor's knife.

He strode from the shop, leaving his audience in open-mouthed awe.

III

By the time Conrad got to the Hill mansion everything lay in deep shadow. He could just discern the outline of the house—that it was quite large and constructed of wood and stone.

He went up to the massive front door and rapped loudly. The sound echoed in the stillness. From somewhere in the woods he heard the barking of dogs. They were obviously big dogs, probably hunting dogs. Conrad peered into the darkness but couldn't see anything. He rapped again. Still no answer. The dogs had come closer. Their bark sounded vicious, and Conrad rapped on the door again, more loudly. At the same time his hand started for the knife.

The door was opened by a delicate-looking man with a fringe of gray hair.

He half shut the door again—

Conrad introduced himself, and after a momentary hesitation the butler ushered him inside, murmuring that the servants' entrance was safe from the dogs.

"When visitors, or guests, are expected," he added, "a light is put over the front door. The dogs know that."

Conrad waited in an ante-room until the butler returned and told him Mr. Hill would see him in his study.

Mr. Benjamin Hill was seated behind a large mahogany desk.

He was broad-shouldered and heavy-set. A bit jowly. Red-faced. He had sharp, businessman's eyes.

In the ashtray in front of him a large black cigar burned slowly.

Conrad handed him a fat envelope, and then waited. Mr. Hill did not ask him to sit down.

Mr. Hill spread out the papers before him. There were numerous letters of recommendation and a very brief autobiographical sketch.

After Mr. Hill had read the sketch, he said, "It seems you have never worked before . . ."

Conrad replied that it had never been necessary.

"And then you were wiped out?"

Conrad shrugged. "For all practical purposes."

"That was several years ago?"

"Yes."

Mr. Hill appraised Conrad's cadaverous figure, and his cheap and severe clothes. "How have you managed till now?"

"Friends."

Mr. Hill pursed his lips but said nothing.

Mr. Hill then sorted out Conrad's letters of recommendation and went through them one by one, very carefully. Several times he returned to a letter he had already read and compared it with the one he was reading. When at last he had finished he looked up at Conrad and said, as though he were thinking out loud:

"Recommendations from chefs of the best restaurants in the City—recommendations from renowned gourmets—from the editor of the journal which carried my advertisement—character references from unimpeachable sources, men whom I myself would consider it a great honor to know on such intimate terms . . ."

Respect, even awe, was in Mr. Hill's voice.

"Sit down, please," Mr. Hill murmured.

But as Conrad continued to stand, Mr. Hill visibly collected himself. He straightened his shoulders and cleared his voice. He seemed to tell himself that he was, after all, only hiring a cook.

"Everything seems to be in order," he said.

From a drawer he took out a letter and glanced at it. "You wrote that you have been a gourmet cook for years, and that you can cook for upwards of twenty people with ease. You can cook both simple fare and elaborate dishes—is that correct?"

Conrad replied that he believed the letters Mr. Hill had just read confirmed that.

"Yes, yes—" Mr. Hill agreed hustily, lowering his eyes.

He finished reading Conrad's letter in silence and then put it into the envelope with the others.

For several seconds he tapped on the desk with the envelope, as if he were trying to come to some decision.

"You find the terms of employment set forth in my notice satisfactory?"

Once again Mr. Hill's voice was business-like.

Conrad said yes, he found them satisfactory.

A few more taps of the envelope and Mr. Hill made up his mind.

He put the envelope away in a drawer.

"I will say a few words about what will be expected . . ."

Conrad would be responsible for the family's breakfast six days a week and for six dinners, though he would probably cook only four, because they dined out about twice a week.

Feeding of the resident staff would also be his responsibility.

The family had breakfast at seven-thirty. Dinner between eight and eight-thirty—the latitude being a concession to the cook.

Once or twice a week they entertained.

On Sunday, dinner was served between one-thirty and two, and after that Conrad's time would be his own. Every night after dinner—they were usually through by nine-thirty—he would also be free. His regular day off was Tuesday.

Conrad would do all of the buying of the food. He would also be in complete charge of the kitchen, though nominally the butler, Maxfield, was his superior.

Mr. Hill stood up.

"You will not be expected to prepare dinner tonight, but breakfast tomorrow morning will be your responsibility. —Do you have any questions?"

Conrad replied that he had two questions; first he asked why the last cook had left.

"He was caught padding the kitchen account. Number two?"

"Does the family have any strong likes or dislikes about food?"

Mr. Hill said no; but the family tended to be heavy, so fattening dishes should be kept to a minimum.

Mr. Hill rang for the butler. "Maxfield will answer any questions you may have about the household."

Mr. Hill took a long puff on his cigar.

"In six months," he said, "I will give you a raise in wages if you prove to be satisfactory."

IV

". . . In the old days I would have been called the house steward. But today I am the butler. My name is Maxfield. I am in charge of the resident staff—of all the resident staff."

Maxfield eyed Conrad coldly from across the narrow table.

"By that I mean—in case you miss my point—*you* are directly answerable to *me*." Again he paused, significantly.

"For what?" Conrad said, returning his gaze.

Maxfield's lips tightened at the question, and then a small quiver appeared at the corner of his mouth.

"The housekeeper, Mrs. Wigton," he continued, choosing not to hear, "is also answerable to me. If on occasion—say, a dinner party—you think you have need of her services in the kitchen, come to me. Do not go to her. I will pass on your request. Her services might be required elsewhere in the house."

Conrad glanced around the small room. It was very tidy, but all the furniture was old and ill-matched.

"This is the housekeeper's room," Maxfield said. "Mrs. Wigton and I take our meals here—after the family has eaten."

"I suppose," Conrad murmured, "my room is even smaller. —Where do the other servants eat?"

Maxfield frowned. "The other members of the staff . . ." he began pompously, but did not continue. He had suddenly turned a sickly shade of gray, and putting both hands to his mouth, sought vainly to smother half a dozen spastic hiccups.

"Indigestion?" Conrad asked.

Maxfield nodded weakly. When he was able to talk again he explained that his was an extremely sensitive stomach and that certain foods simply did not agree with him. Paul, the temporary cook, knew this, but disregarded it completely. Indeed, only the day before, Maxfield had been forced to take to his bed after eating one of Paul's vile concoctions.

Maxfield proceeded with his briefing.

The other members of the staff—Betsy, the maid; Rudolph, the footman; and Eggy, the kitchen boy—ate in the kitchen.

Conrad would be responsible for all the food purchases. Whether he did the actual buying was up to him. Paul usually sent Eggy into town, or Rudolph when he could be spared.

Conrad would keep a strict account of all expenditures.

"And now I'll show you your room."

At the rear of the mansion, wooden steps led up to the third floor.

As Conrad had expected, his room was small. It contained a table, a chair and a narrow bed—about a foot too short for Conrad.

Maxfield noticed the discrepancy and murmured that he

would suggest that Master Harold speak to one of the carpenters at the mill.

"Where is the kitchen?" Conrad asked.

"We were just going there."

On the way Maxfield advised him that Paul was not only a poor cook—he was also a terrible gossip. Nothing he said should be believed. He exaggerated and made things up. Conrad would do well to turn a deaf ear.

When they entered the kitchen Paul looked up from the stove—and dropped his ladle, so startled was he by the tall, gaunt figure in black.

"This is the new cook," Maxfield told Paul curtly. "And over there," he continued to Conrad, "is Eggy, your kitchen boy. Eggy!"

Eggy was slowly washing dishes. He turned around.

"This is your new master," Maxfield told him

Eggy squinted across the kitchen, and grinned.

"Yes, sir," he mumbled. "Yes, sir."

"He's short-sighted and short-minded," Maxfield said. "You can go back to your work now, Eggy."

"Yes, sir."

"Eggy likes his work . . ."

Smiling nervously, Paul started toward Conrad, evidently with some notion of shaking hands. But seeing Conrad look right through him and make no move to uncross his arms, he thought better of it.

Paul was a youngish man with carroty-red hair and a snub nose. His skin had been bleached white by kitchen steams.

"If you want to get your things—" Maxfield began, but Conrad ignored him, and brushing past Paul, who had to side-step quickly, went over to the stove and examined the burners and the oven.

In answer to his question, Paul said the stove was in perfect working order.

Maxfield lingered by the door. Obviously he did not want to leave Conrad alone with Paul, and so Conrad began questioning Paul about the kitchen facilities. After about fifteen minutes the buzzer above the door sounded, and Maxfield left.

Conrad then started asking Paul about the food he prepared for the Hills.

No, he never made any pies or cakes. All pastries came from town. No, he never made any soups. The Hills didn't like them. No, he never made any sauces—just a little meat gravy.

Fish? No, the family never asked him to serve fish. They seemed to get enough of that at the Vale mansion. Brogg, the Vale cook, was famous for his fish dishes. No one was expected to compete with him. Moreover, the only really good fish came from the Vale lakes and was never available in the fish markets in Cobb—Brogg and Mr. Vale saw to that.

"What do you prepare for breakfast?"

Paul replied that it was always the same: ham and eggs, cereal, toast and coffee.

"Lunch?"

"Sandwiches. Betsy makes them—"

"And for dinner?"

Paul wrinkled his snub nose. "Mostly I give them a salad, meat, one vegetable, potatoes—boiled or mashed—and fruit or ice cream afterwards."

"Do you serve them that every night?" Conrad asked disgustedly.

"Yes, sir," Paul admitted. "It's not that I can't cook. I like to cook, but Mr. and Mrs. Hill don't care for anything fancy. They always say they don't want to be experimented on—"

Conrad cut him off. "Do they have large appetites?"

The young man answered with long, slow nods. "They eat like horses, sir."

Conrad took the ladle from Paul's hand, dipped out a little of the broth in which the meat was cooking—and went to the sink and spat it into Eggy's dishwater. —"And with the taste, apparently, of pigs."

"I don't suppose it's very good—"

"Who interferes in the kitchen?"

"Only Mrs. Wigton, the old hen. She tries to tell me how to do the cooking—she used to be a cook a long time ago."

"None of the family sticks his nose in the kitchen?"

Paul shook his head.

"Never?"

"Well, after there have been guests for dinner Mrs. Hill usually stops by and says she appreciates all the work I did and hopes it won't take me too long to get the kitchen cleaned up."

"And the daughter . . . ?" Conrad began looking in all the cupboards.

"No. Ester is a real beauty but she's haughty. I almost never see her. But Harold's okay. He's not like his sister. He's friendly. Sometimes he drops in to ask me how I'm doing, and he smells whatever I have cooking and he always says it smells good. And sometimes he asks me questions, about how I made something . . ."

"And Mr. Hill?"

Paul yelled at Eggy to start peeling some potatoes, and then told Conrad that Mr. Hill dropped in about once a week to pass the time of day. "He's very busy overseeing the mill and the estate," he explained. "He doesn't have much time for anything else. Harold helps him, but he doesn't seem to be very interested—he stays at home most of the day doing nothing. I think Mr. Hill is disappointed . . ."

Conrad had seen and heard enough. "Do you go to any tavern in Cobb?"

Paul ran his hand through his red hair.

"I don't drink much, sir. But when I do I go to Ben's. That's where most of the domestics go. The only other place they go is to the White Door, but there are too many fights there."

"All right, I can reach you at Ben's then," Conrad said, and stepping around Eggy, who was bent over a bucket of potatoes, he went out the kitchen door.

V

Later that night, after the servants and the family had retired and the house was quiet, Conrad went to the kitchen and warmed up some meat he had brought in his rucksack. While he ate he set some dough, and then he went outside and walked around to the side of the house, alert for the sound of dogs.

The moon had come up, and far away the Prominence was outlined against the purple sky. Even from that distance its Gothic mass dominated the landscape.

Conrad sat down on the damp grass and looked at the Prominence.

He stayed there for about an hour, until he began to feel the chill; then he strolled once around the house and returned to his room.

Conrad had just finished buttering the muffin pan when the kitchen door opened and a squat, sour-faced woman entered.

Though Mrs. Wigton had been apprised by Maxfield of Conrad's unusual appearance, she nonetheless started at the sight of him. She had pictured him in black, whereas now he was all in white, and wearing a great chef's hat that made him look nine feet tall.

But recovering: "I'm Mrs. Wigton," she informed him, "the housekeeper."

"I'm Conrad, the cook," he returned. "What do you want?"

Flustered both by the question and the menacing coldness with which it was asked, Mrs. Wigton muttered something about just thinking they should get to know each other.

Conrad replied there would be plenty of time for that if it should prove necessary, which he doubted. He added that if she had no other business with him she could return to her duties, and henceforth would be well advised to stay clear of the kitchen.

Mortified, Mrs. Wigton huffed and declared she would speak to her mistress.

A little later Eggy appeared. Conrad told him he was late. He wanted him in the kitchen by six-thirty, and asked where he slept. Eggy stuttered out that he slept in the shed behind the house, with Rudolph. Conrad said that if he didn't get up on time he himself would wake him, rudely, and then he told Eggy to begin rewashing all the dishes—they were streaked and dirty. He should change the dishwater more often and use a little elbow grease.

Eggy, who had begun to quake as Conrad berated him, set to with rather more of a will than he had evinced the evening before.

By the time Betsy came in, breakfast was just about ready. Conrad made only one innovation in the meal Paul had described: instead of making toast he baked some muffins.

Betsy looked the typical maid-of-all-work—a simple-minded slattern of indeterminate years. Her uniform was ill-fitting, the lace more gray than white, her cap without starch.

"Wash your hands," Conrad snapped, without so much as a glance at them, "twice, and with soap."

But Betsy just looked at the startling figure before her.

Conrad pointed: "In the sink."

For a moment the girl continued to stand there, then curtsied gracelessly and ran to the sink.

While she scrubbed her hands, Conrad asked her several questions about how she served—pointed and simple questions, requiring only a yes or no. He explained a few changes, made sure she understood, and then told her breakfast was ready.

He looked her hands over before she left—except for the nails they were clean—and he told her not to put her fingers in the food, promising to cut them off if he ever caught her at it.

Betsy, tray in hand, executed another curtsy . . .

While the family ate, Conrad fixed breakfast for Mrs. Wigton and Maxfield. Mrs. Wigton got the same as the family, but for Maxfield he prepared a bland gruel and a very light custard.

Betsy made several trips to the kitchen, curtsying each time until Conrad told her to stop.

"Is the family eating heartily?" he asked her on one of her trips.

"Yes, sir."

"Have they said anything?"

"You mean, whether they like it?" Betsy asked, her eyes bright with comprehension. "No, sir. But I think they do, because they're eating all of it . . ."

"Like pigs," Conrad muttered to himself.

Betsy looked hungrily at the food Conrad had prepared for the housekeeper and the butler. "Should I take breakfast to the housekeeper's room?" she asked timidly.

"Do they usually eat breakfast before the family finishes?"

"Yes, sir."

As Betsy left, she nearly bumped into an ox-like figure in bright-red livery who suddenly loomed in the doorway, completely filling it.

"I'm Rudolph," the figure announced, looking at Conrad.

Conrad told him to get out of the way so Betsy could get past him.

Rudolph obliged quickly, coming into the kitchen.

He showed no surprise at the sight of Conrad. Indeed, there was no discernable expression on his face—just a face with features, exceptional only in their bluntness. Brown hair straggled down over a brutishly low forehead.

"I'm hungry," Rudolph declared.

Conrad almost smiled.

"Well, you've come to the right place. What would you like to eat, my good man?"

Rudolph hesitated—as if he were not used to being asked.

"Anything," he said at last; "whatever there is."

Conrad told him to sit in the corner, and then got out a large bowl. He had cooked the scraps left from last night's dinner into a kind of mush; he ladled this into the bowl and handed it to Rudolph. Rudolph, after sniffing it, began eating ravenously.

He served the same to Eggy.

When Betsy came back he also gave her a bowl of the mush, but just as she started to eat the buzzer sounded.

She returned at once, saying that Mrs. Hill would like to know if there were any more muffins . . .

After breakfast a tall, statuesque woman came into the kitchen. "I'm Mrs. Hill," she smiled, concealing her surprise at Conrad's appearance. "I just wanted to tell you that your muffins were delicious."

Conrad inclined his head and thanked her.

And before Mrs. Hill left: "Could we possibly have some more muffins for breakfast tomorrow morning?"

VI

After paying a second visit to the three butchers, Conrad decided to buy his meat from Albert's Butcher Shop, where he had thrown the leg of mutton on the floor.

The butcher remembered him, and seeing Eggy trailing in his wake: "You are the Hills' new cook? I'm glad to see you again."

Albert was a porcine-faced man with greedy eyes. His eyes were the principal reason Conrad had decided to patronize him.

Conrad examined all the meat in the case and then demanded to be taken to the storage room. Albert said there was nothing back there that wasn't in the case, but as Conrad turned to leave the shop he quickly relented.

Conrad at last found something that would do, but Albert

said it was impossible—it would mean ruining several other cuts from the large piece of meat. Conrad said it was either that or nothing.

After Albert had cut it—with assistance from Conrad, who had taken the knife from his hand and outlined precisely the piece he wanted—he named the price of the meat. Conrad told him he wouldn't pay it . . .

"But after I've cut it—" the man whined.

Conrad told him to eat it himself, and ordered Eggy to follow him.

Albert followed him to the door, sniveling and protesting— and not till Conrad was already outside the shop did he ask Conrad how much he would pay. When Conrad told him Albert raised his eyes to heaven and began protesting with even greater vehemence. But Conrad replied that he would still be making a robber's profit . . .

While Albert wrapped the meat for him, Conrad decided on his own dinner and said he wanted two chicken breasts. Albert declared he did not sell chicken parts. Conrad retorted that he would then buy all of the poultry for the Hill household at one of Albert's competitors', and probably all of the meat too.

". . . and now I want some bones," Conrad said after they had settled on a considerably reduced price for the chicken breasts, "and several pounds of meat scraps—what *I* call meat scraps."

For the large package of bones and scraps, which Eggy shouldered along with the roast and chicken, Conrad paid nothing at all.

Before Conrad had gone shopping that morning Maxfield had come into the kitchen, and it was immediately evident that his manner had greatly changed from the night before.

He thanked Conrad for his special breakfast. He said it was very considerate of him.

He also said that Mrs. Wigton had been terribly put out with Conrad, but that as she ate her breakfast her ire had slowly subsided. For one thing, her breakfast wasn't cold, as it had usually been when Paul was the cook. And for another, it wasn't just thrown on the plate in any which way. And for another, the muffins. She admitted they were delicious.

"And I agree with her on that," Maxfield said with a shy smile, the first he had vouchsafed Conrad. "She let me have a half of one . . ."

Conrad looked disapproving. "I didn't fix you a special breakfast to have you undo it by eating something not meant for you."

Conrad was probably the only person who had ever shown him any genuine concern, and the old butler hung his head sheepishly.

"Now, there's one thing," Conrad continued; "those dogs . . ."

He said he had been looking around near the edge of the woods for a place to plant some herbs when the dogs had suddenly appeared and set upon him. Whose responsibility were they?

Maxfield said they were Master Harold's dogs. They were vicious brutes, and friendly to no one but Harold. Only he could do anything with them but he really didn't like them. They had been given to him by his godfather, Mr. Vale, and that was the only reason he kept them.

"Who feeds them?"

Maxfield replied that no one fed them. They hunted for their food.

"What about the left-overs from the kitchen?"

The butler smiled understandingly. "The cook has always thrown them whatever scraps he thought they would eat but that has never made them like the cook any better. They're strange beasts."

Conrad said people simply didn't know how to feed dogs.

"And the daughter, Ester," he added; "Betsy says she has cats . . ."

Maxfield nodded. "Given to her by her godmother, Mrs. Vale."

When Conrad had returned from shopping he put some of the bones and scraps and other odds and ends in a large pot and let the mess boil while he started preparations for dinner.

Just as the sun was setting he saw the dogs in the back sniffing around the refuse containers, and threw them some of the bones he had cooked. A paste-like substance had been left in the pot, and from that he had made a few dozen round balls. As the dogs worried the bones, snarling both at each other and at Conrad, who had sat down on the back steps, he rolled three or four of the balls toward them. At first they must have thought he was playing, because they ignored the balls completely. But then their noses corrected this impression, and they retrieved the balls and ate them. Then Conrad rolled a few more, and they left the bones and ran after the balls, still snarling. Conrad continued to roll the balls until they had eaten them all.

The next afternoon the dogs reappeared about the same time, and Conrad went out again with the bones and the balls, only this time the dogs retrieved the balls as soon as he started rolling them.

This performance was repeated on successive days until the dogs no longer snarled as they went after the balls.

Soon it became a game, and the dogs learned to catch the balls in the air.

Then one afternoon Conrad had Eggy throw them some of the balls, though Eggy was terrified of the dogs.

But after a few days it became a game for Eggy; Conrad would only throw one ball to each dog and Eggy would throw the rest.

VII

And while Conrad was taming the dogs, he was also becoming acquainted with their master:

". . . it smelled so good I just had to come in. I was walking around the back . . ."

Conrad looked up from his labors to see a tall, broad-shouldered young man standing by the back door.

"I'm Harold . . ."

As they shook hands Harold asked him what he was fixing for dinner.

"I'm marinating a roast," Conrad replied, "but what I believe you smell is the dog food cooking."

Harold's eyes widened. "Really?" He peered into the pot, and then laughed pleasantly. "I rather envy the dogs."

Harold's manner was very easy. Remarking that he would only disturb Conrad for a few minutes, he sat down on the high stool by the sink—Eggy's stool. Conrad noted a slightly dreamy look in the young man's eyes. Other than that, he was very good-looking—strong features, high forehead, thick blond hair. And when he took out his pipe and lit it, Conrad saw that he had long, sensitive fingers.

Conrad continued with his work, and Harold watched him without saying anything.

At last Harold stood up: "Maxfield spoke to me about your bed. The men are working on the new one now. It's seven feet long—they may have to move it into your room in sections."

Conrad thanked him, and added that he was getting tired of sleeping on the floor.

Harold had imagined that Conrad slept in the bed somehow, and when Conrad told him this he was visibly taken aback. He promised that the bed would be delivered the very next day.

He was true to his word.

After the workmen had installed the bed, Harold lingered in the room: Conrad was starting to open two large packing crates which had arrived that morning.

The crates revealed an incredible collection of books, all sizes and ages. Many were in foreign languages, and as Harold helped Conrad unpack them his curiosity grew.

"They're all cook books," Conrad explained.

Harold looked dumbfounded.

Conrad said he read cook books all the time, especially at night.

Besides the books there were dozens of folders jammed with cut-out recipes.

Examining the books, Harold noticed all kinds of marginal notations in them. Conrad told him they were his notes—emendations, additions, cross-references to his other books, etc. Somewhat in awe Harold asked if he had ever compiled a cook book himself, and Conrad showed him stacks of loose-leaf note-books full of close-written, cryptic formulae—special recipes and methods of his own conceiving.

The books seemed to cover every subject. In addition to the general cook books there were speciality books—books on sauces, marinades, individual cuts of meat, different kinds of meat, game, fish, fowl, particular vegetables, eggs, cheeses, wine dishes, beer dishes, summer dishes, winter dishes, salads, casseroles, pies, cakes, puddings, icings. There were also books for special kinds of diets.

There was even a book on cat food.

Harold became more impressed by the minute.

"I didn't know there were that many cook books in the world," he marveled.

Conrad showed him a directory of book dealers who would search out any kind of cook book he ordered.

He also showed him an address book of establishments all over the world which handled specialty-food items. Beside each address there were examples of their inventory.

"One can send for all those things," Conrad explained.

Harold was so intrigued by the new world he had discovered that he didn't even notice Conrad leave . . .

After dinner that night Harold dropped by the kitchen to congratulate Conrad on the roast and the sauce he had served with it.

"I've never tasted anything like it," he said.

And as he left: "You'll need some book shelves in your room. I'll get one of the men at the mill to start making them tomorrow."

VIII

Not only Albert, the butcher, but also the fishmongers, the greengrocers and the old, bearded provisioner of canned goods discovered Conrad to be a sharp and imperious shopper. Of course his accounts reflected this, and when Maxfield went over them that first Sunday morning he was openly astounded.

"When does Mrs. Hill go over the accounts?" Conrad asked.

"This afternoon—Mrs. Hill, Mrs. Wigton and I." The old butler sighed. "Sunday is not a day of rest around here, except for Ester. Mr. Hill and Harold go to the mill and examine those accounts. 'Sunday afternoon,' as Mr. and Mrs. Hill always say, 'is accounting time.'"

"And Betsy and Rudolph?"

"They polish silver."

"And Eggy?"

"Eggy is yours. The cook usually has him clean the stove."

"The stove is already clean. —And the cook?"

Maxfield smiled wanly.

"Theoretically the cook is free Sunday afternoon. But he must be available—in case there are any questions about his accounts."

Conrad, who had been busy stuffing a goose, looked around. "*Must*, did you say?"

Maxfield hesitated, and then admitted that perhaps *should* would be a better word.

"I suspect *won't* would be the best," Conrad rejoined, resuming his work on the stuffing. Before Maxfield could reply Betsy came in, looking put upon and muttering something about Miss Ester's cats.

It was her duty to open the cans of cat food and empty the contents into three dishes, then take the dishes up to the cats in Ester's room. It was the one complaint she had about her job.

". . . those cats!" she grumbled, getting the cans from the bottom of the cupboard. "They're fat and lazy, and their hair gets over everything. I don't see why I have to feed them. I'd like to put them in a bag and put some rocks in the bag and tie up the end with some string and throw them in Blue Lake. That's where they belong. They're good for nothing. They don't even play."

The last time Conrad had gone shopping he had got some fish heads. He had made stock from these and mixed it with dough, which he then worked into small mice.

When Betsy had finished dumping the canned cat food into the dishes, Conrad pointed to several ramekins which contained the mice swimming in a light cream sauce, and told her they were also for the cats and that she should take them with her. Betsy was very surprised at the sight of the mice, and as if they were something for her to play with, she started to touch one. Conrad sharply ordered her to keep her fingers off.

"Are the cats supposed to eat them?" she inquired timidly, still staring at the little mice.

"Just carry them upstairs. If your mistress says anything, tell her they're the cats' special Sunday dinner. —On Sunday there is special food for all."

After Betsy had left, Maxfield murmured that he doubted whether Miss Ester would let the cats eat what Conrad had made. "She never lets them eat anything from the kitchen."

"She will make an exception this time," Conrad said as he put the goose in the oven. "The cats will scratch her to shreds if she tries to take those mice away."

Sunday dinner was served precisely at 1:45, with Conrad himself carrying the goose. Betsy followed him with the vegetables.

Sighs of appreciation rose from the family and they also looked pleased with the vision of their cook, all in white and more than seven feet tall in his chef's hat. Out of the corner of his eye Conrad saw Ester. She was blond and beautiful. But he didn't look directly at her, so he couldn't tell whether she had sighed at the sight of the glistening brown goose with its colorful garnishings.

Conrad had learned from Maxfield that Mr. Hill did not carve well and did not relish the chore; therefore he had started the carving himself. But he had done this so carefully and with such a thin knife that the slicing could not be detected unless one got very close to the goose and looked for it.

Conrad set the goose in front of Mr. Hill, who sat at the head of the table, and then stood beside him and folded his arms. Dramatically he waited till everyone had looked at the goose for about half a minute, and then he murmured to Mr. Hill that with his permission he would begin the carving. Mr. Hill, a trifle awed at the sight of the beautiful and succulent-looking bird, and doubtless a bit uneasy at the prospect of carving it—or mutilating it—quickly nodded assent. Conrad picked up the knife and with a flourish severed a marvelous slice of meat, and then a second. Mr. Hill observed him closely, trying to see how it was done. Conrad put the two slices on a plate, and while the eyes of the rest of the family followed the slices, Conrad took the knife and revealed to the surprised Mr. Hill that the difficult part of the carving had already been done.

Mr. Hill smiled as Conrad handed him the knife . . .

Conrad waited until Mr. Hill reached the stuffing.

"The stuffing," he said, and all eyes turned to him at the sound of his voice, "is sausage and chestnut, though chestnuts, one is told, cannot be procured at this time of year. But the manageress of one of the greengroceries was persuaded to look."

He paused, and Mrs. Hill laughed lightly.

"Conrad, word has already spread about how you browbeat the local shopkeepers. Indeed, I've had one or two complaints . . ." She sounded extremely pleased.

"And you will probably get more," Conrad murmured. He continued, "It is a rich stuffing. Therefore the vegetables are quite plain. Except for the peas, I have prepared no sauces for them. The peas are in thin white sauce. As for the other vegetables, I would not advise putting any of the gravy on them. The gravy goes best on the meat itself, and perhaps a little on the stuffing."

He added that a light dessert would follow, and then withdrew.

＊＊＊

Conrad was eating some dumplings cooked in the goose fat when Maxfield came in. A peculiar expression was on the butler's face, and his first words revealed that something out of the ordinary had transpired: Mrs. Hill had retired to her room and had postponed the accounts until the following day.

Moreover, Mr. Hill had not gone to the mill. Instead he had gone to his study, and he was now asleep in his chair with his feet cocked up on his desk.

And Master Harold was stretched out asleep on the divan in the living room.

Conrad pointed to the ravaged remains of the goose carcass, and said it wasn't surprising they were asleep, since they had eaten so much.

"Only Ester seems to be awake," Maxfield muttered, shaking his head in bewilderment, "and she usually sleeps Sunday afternoon."

Conrad asked Maxfield how he had enjoyed his chicken. He apologized for not mentioning it, but it had been heavenly. It was the best chicken he had ever eaten, and it was sitting perfectly on his stomach. He added that Mrs. Wigton had requested him to convey her appreciation of the chops. She would have come herself but she was not sure of the reception she would get . . .

The old butler repeated his apologies for not telling Conrad how much he had enjoyed his dinner, ". . . but I was so surprised to see all of the family sleeping. I cannot recall such a thing ever happening before . . ."

Just then Betsy came in. "They didn't even touch their cat food!" she exclaimed. "They just ate the little mice!"

❧

Conrad had set Sunday afternoon aside to explore some of the lakes. Since the Vales were coming to dinner on Wednesday, he wished to have fish for them—after all, hadn't he been told their cook was peerless in his preparation of fish? And therefore the

Vales were doubtless connoisseurs of fish. A skillfully prepared fish should please them no end.

With luck he might encounter some men who would do a little poaching . . .

IX

On his day off Conrad met the fishermen in Ben's tavern, as had been arranged. Money and fish changed hands, and the men told him that any time he wanted some fish he should just leave a message for them at Ben's.

Conrad left and made the rounds of the other taverns, drinking a beer or two in each one.

There were five taverns in all, and Conrad decided the last one was most to his liking. It had a cellar drinking room, with old wooden tables and benches. There was a small kitchen in the rear. Upstairs a few rooms were to let.

The Shepard's Inn was run by a stout middle-aged woman, indifferently assisted by a short, lame man who passed for her husband.

Both complained that business was bad.

Conrad asked to look at the rooms. He said he was the Hills'
cook and that he wanted a permanent room in town. The woman,
Nell, said she knew who he was. Some of the shopkeepers had
spoken of him. She implied that what they had said wasn't exactly favorable. Then she told him the price.

Conrad said he would take a room on a permanent basis, but
at a quarter of the rent she was asking.

"No," the woman said, "I've heard of you. You're not going to
get me to give you anything free."

Conrad pointed out that he wasn't asking for the room free.
He ordered another beer.

"Will you drink here," Nell asked finally, "when you come
into town?"

Conrad said he would.

As he handed her the first week's rent he told her some boxes
would arrive shortly from the City, which should be put in his
room. They contained mostly clothes. He would appreciate it
if she would hang the clothes in the closet.

Nell folded her fat arms and leaned on the bar.

"The price of the room doesn't include maid service. Perhaps
if you'd pay a decent rent . . ."

Conrad finished his stein of beer without replying. But as he
turned to leave: "I would have had another one," he explained,
fixing her with his black eyes, "or perhaps six more. It would
cost you nothing to hang up my clothes. I can only conclude
you're a stupid woman. —And soon," he continued, emphasizing
each word, "people will come here because I come here. And
when I stop coming here, they will stop coming here. And in
case the significance eludes you: when that day comes you will
beg me to stay in your room rent-free."

". . . I paid some men to poach it from the Vale lakes."

Mrs. Hill's eyes brightened with understanding. "Well, I knew it must have been something like that. Mr. and Mrs. Vale simply could not understand it—they insisted the fish was out of season and not available at any price. And, Conrad, you should have seen their faces when they took the first mouthful! And the looks they exchanged . . ."

Mrs. Hill leaned back on Conrad's stool and closed her eyes, reliving the delightful experience.

"You know," she went on after a moment, "they think they have the best cook in the world. Only Brogg can prepare fish to suit them. But even though I could see it galled them, they had to admit they'd never eaten anything finer, and they're both very finicky eaters—in delicate health, you know. So thin. They've been that way for years."

Conrad said that if he were given a few days' notice he believed he could get whatever fish the lakes had in them, and he asked if the Vales were especially fond of any dish.

Mrs. Hill nodded and said there were several, but one in particular, which she named and tried to describe. "They insist that only Brogg can make it."

Conrad merely shrugged at that.

"I don't know whether you know any of the family history," Mrs. Hill continued in a slightly intimate voice, "but for years and years the Hills and Vales feuded. Over what, I'm not sure even they knew. But now we are more civilized and we only feud"—Mrs. Hill smiled as she said this—"over our cooks. And for some time now, ever since they lured Brogg away from the Morton family in Highlands, I fear they have been getting the better of the feud. Perhaps the tide of battle is about to change."

The next day when Conrad went shopping he left two messages at Ben's: one for Paul, the Hills' previous cook, and one for the two fishermen, who later that evening appeared at the back door.

"Who were those men?" Maxfield asked when Conrad came back into the kitchen. "I heard what the Vales said last night at dinner," he continued when Conrad ignored his question, "and if Brogg ever finds out that you hired poachers to get fish from his lakes . . ."

Conrad cut him short: "What did Mrs. Hill say about my accounts?"

"I didn't show them to her. I decided to wait until you have been here two weeks. That way the picture will be more reliable. —But let me warn you, Brogg is a bad man to have for an enemy . . ."

"Do you know," Conrad broke in again, "there is not a complete set of china or glassware in this house? I've seen Betsy break seven plates, four glasses and two cups. Even Eggy hasn't broken that many. Is it the butler's or the housekeeper's responsibility to see that a decent serving set exists? And I don't mean perfect, just decent. It is impossible to entertain with our mutilated remains."

Slowly the old butler's neck and face turned red. "Whoever's responsibility it is," he replied in a trembling voice, "it is not yours."

The two men glared at each other, and then Maxfield turned and stalked out, his lips still trembling.

"Mind your ulcers," Conrad called after him.

After dinner Conrad was in the kitchen, shaping a crown roast for next day's meal, when he heard a scratching at the door. He opened it, and a large cream-colored cat streaked in from the dining room and began sniffing around the legs of the worktable.

Conrad was just contemplating chucking it out the back door when a quick rap sounded and Ester walked in, followed by her brother a few steps behind.

"I was right," she said; "there's Queen Bee III." She went over and picked up the cat. "Naughty, naughty kitty," she intoned, stroking it.

"I hope we haven't disturbed you," Harold apologized.

Conrad resumed his labors.

"You made those delicious mice, didn't you?" Ester said, seeming to notice Conrad for the first time. It sounded as if she had eaten the mice herself. "Will you make some more—this Sunday?"

"No."

Ester frowned. "No?" she repeated.

"I'm going to make some birds."

"Oh!"

For a moment Ester looked puzzled, and then: "Did you hear that, kitty? You're going to have some nice birds this Sunday."

Ester looked at Conrad again. "Do you know anything about feeding cats?"

"Ester," Harold exclaimed, "of course he does! He has a whole book on cat food."

"You have? Well, some day when I have time, you'll have to tell me all about it. —Come on, kitty. It's time we went to bed . . ."

Very diffidently Harold asked whether he might stay a few minutes and watch Conrad work. Conrad replied that he was nearly through, and as he put the finishing touches on the crown he explained what he was doing. Harold was most interested.

At last Conrad put the roast away, and then Harold said he had something he wanted to ask him: a week from Saturday the employees at the mill were going on their annual red-bird hunt. In the evening they would have an outdoor feast. Charles, the cook they had hired for the past few years, had recently been made chef at the Prominence Inn and could not be spared. Brogg had been telling everybody that he would be the cook on red-bird night—that the Hills would be forced to come to him. But Brogg always got into fights when he drank—and so, would Conrad be willing to take Charles's place? He would be recompensed handsomely.

Conrad said he had no objections. "How do the men like their red-birds?"

Harold described, vaguely, how the birds were usually prepared, but said Conrad would have a free hand.

"I will be in complete charge of all preparations?"

"Yes."

The following Tuesday Conrad went to his room at the Shepard's Inn. The boxes from the city had arrived and his clothes were hanging neatly in the closet.

"I hope you appreciate what I did for you," Nell said when he went downstairs for a beer.

Conrad replied that she hadn't done anything for him. "You just pursued your self-interest. What I appreciate is your ability to recognize it. —I suppose you know this Saturday is red-bird night for the Hill employees?"

"What of it?"

"They drink a lot of beer, don't they?"

"That means nothing to me," Nell replied, making a sour face and producing in the process another chin or two from her ample neck. "Charles orders all the beer from the Prominence Inn—and gets a cut too, I'm sure."

Conrad waited till she had finished grumbling, and then told her that news must travel slow. "I'm the cook for red-bird night, and I'm doing all the ordering."

When that had soaked in he asked for another stein—and neglected to put any money on the bar.

"I'm expecting a friend," Conrad said, "and we are going to discuss the ordering of beer. He will tell me where I can get the best bargain."

At this Nell looked distressed. She said she would sell him the beer very cheap, and she named the price per keg. Conrad laughed at the figure.

Long before Paul arrived Nell had agreed to Conrad's terms, which included a month's free rent.

Conrad bought Paul a beer and explained why he had left the message at Ben's: on his day off he always planned to dine in town, at the Prominence Inn, and he wanted Paul to make certain arrangements for him. He would have to talk to the head waiter and to the cook—did he know Charles?

"I've known him for years," Paul answered. "He recommended me for the present job I have with the Renfrews. He's a very good cook, second only to Brogg."

"If you take a recipe to him, will he follow the directions to the letter?"

Paul wrinkled his snub nose. "I'm not sure I know what you mean, but I suppose if you pay him he will."

"I'll pay him. Do they have private dining rooms there?"

"They have one, but I don't think anyone ever uses it."

Paul's wonderment continued to grow as Conrad explained what he wanted him to do.

After about an hour—with a small packet of Conrad's money in his pocket, some very specific instructions in his head, and several carefully detailed recipes in his hand—Paul stood up. It was getting late. "The Renfrews have only a maid and I have to do the shopping myself."

Conrad suggested they start shopping together. "I will show you how to get your accounts down."

Paul looked pleased. He said Mrs. Renfrew had already told him he was spending too much. "She's worse than Mrs. Hill. But from the things I've heard the shopkeepers say about you, I don't suppose you've had a run-in with her over the accounts."

Conrad admitted that was true. "Quite the contrary. And by

the way, she no longer does the accounts on Sunday. She sleeps, as does the rest of the family. Only Ester stays awake, playing with the cats."

As Paul left, his expression said plainly that wonders would never cease.

Conrad stayed at the Shepard's Inn, drinking until late at night.

He had brought with him a jar of tangy paté, and had set it on the bar with some crackers.

"That's not for you," he told Nell, who was looking greedily at the paté. "It's for the customers—if any come in here . . . I'm expecting two friends."

Conrad drank by himself until the fishermen arrived.

"Drinks, Nell!" he called. "And put this package on ice . . ."

And after Conrad had bought the men a few more rounds: "Do you do any hunting?" he asked. "Or do you know anyone who does? I need some birds . . ."

X

All day long the open land beyond the mill rang with the firing of guns, and the shouts and laughter of men drinking and having a good time. The shooting was excellent, and in a steady stream the men repaired to the cooking camp at the edge of the wood, exchanging their bags of red-birds for more beer, and then returning to the shoot. The men declared the beer had never been more plentiful.

Toward the end of the day the trips back to the camp became more frequent; though fewer birds were brought in, more beer was taken out . . .

Conrad and his staff worked without let-up. They kept the beer exceedingly cold, and new kegs were always tapped and ready. The birds were also attended to immediately. There were vats of boiling water with great fires beneath them, and plenty of cut wood to keep them going. The birds were plunged into the water, then plucked and seared and made ready for cleaning. After that they became Conrad's responsibility.

It was tradition on red-bird night that a member of the Hill family help feed the men. Harold, of course, had volunteered, and Conrad worked him every bit as hard as he worked Eggy and Rudolph, possibly harder. "One learns from work," Conrad would say as Harold began to draw another dozen birds.

Harold was too busy to answer.

He carefully saved the tiny hearts and livers, which Conrad mixed with berries for the stuffing. The men had never had stuffed birds before. They were also surprised to see Conrad wrap them with strips of salt pork. Prepared thus, the birds were set in a deep tray half full of wine and meat broth, to marinate until the men were all through shooting. Then the trays had only to be slipped into the huge outdoor oven. A small fire had been kept going beneath it since midafternoon, so it would not take long to stoke it to high heat.

Eatingtime was set for about an hour after sundown.

❧

The great fire beneath the oven, and the lesser fires which ringed the dining area and obscured the black forest and hills, consumed wood almost as fast as Rudolph supplied it. Frantically he ran back and forth, his bright red livery making him look rather like a moving torch. Then at one point he stumbled and pitched full-length, scattering an armload of wood among the feet of a tableful of diners.

"Too much beer!" laughed one of the men, kicking some of the small logs toward Rudolph.

Rudolph got up and brushed off his uniform.

"He's been drinking all day!" laughed another man.

"He's drunk more than anyone!" cried a third.

Rudolph recovered all of the wood, and then looked stupidly at the last man who had addressed him.

"I have not," he mumbled. And then, after a moment: "Conrad has. He has drunk the most. I've seen him."

The man started to laugh and say something, but Rudolph added, "Conrad can drink more than anyone. He can even drink more than you, Heavy."

Rudolph turned and flung the wood on the fire.

"Hey, what did you say?" demanded Heavy. "What did you say . . . ?"

And that's how the match came about.

On red-bird night an eating contest was traditional. But for several years this tradition had not been observed for the simple reason that there was no competition: one man, Heavy, had demonstrated time and time again that he could eat twice as many red-birds as any other man.

But Rudolph's words suggested a contest, or perhaps only a good joke.

Heavy and a delegation of men approached Conrad and told him about the tradition. They repeated what they'd heard and inquired whether his capacity extended equally to solid food.

"I have a good appetite," Conrad laughed.

"Wonderful!" exclaimed the men, nudging Heavy and winking at him.

But then Conrad added that it was an insult to good food to engage in deliberate gluttony.

However, more and more men began to clamor for a contest and they wouldn't let Conrad out of it.

After all the others had eaten, Conrad and Heavy sat down at opposite ends of a long table. In front of each was an entire tray of birds, and beside it, an empty tray for bones. Steins of cold beer were on their right.

"Eggy," Conrad said, "I want you to keep my stein full."

Heavy slapped his stomach and gave the same order to Eggy, remarking jovially that he was even more thirsty than hungry.

The maximum time allowed for eating a bird was agreed on, and the match began midst the laughter and shouting of the men who had gathered round the table. Some of them had done a little betting and they encouraged their favorite.

Harold stood behind Conrad, smiling and tired.

At a nearby table two men worked carefully on the prize.

Rudolph, more and more drunk, lurched dutifully from fire to fire.

The match was really over when each man had eaten half his tray of birds and Conrad told Harold to put two more trays in the oven.

Heavy looked across at him, stupified. One tray was his limit and the standing record for the contest.

By the time they started on their last row of birds the outcome had become obvious to all. Heavy was stuffing himself, forcing the birds down. His fat face was beginning to look apoplectic, whereas Conrad was laughing and talking, eating leisurely and delighting in every mouthful.

The ring of men drew closer . . .

At last there was only one bird left on each tray. Heavy picked his up and looked at it. He started to open his mouth. But then he had to close it to keep from gagging.

He tossed the bird on the tray of bones beside him.

A murmur rose from the men.

Conrad laughed and sank his teeth into the breast of his last red-bird.

Everyone began shouting and clapping him on the back.

"The winner! The winner!" they cried. "Conrad's the winner!"

Conrad nodded in acknowledgment, slowly masticating his mouthful of red-bird breast.

And then there were shouts of "The prize! The prize!"

Two men came forward, bearing on a tray a wreath of red-bird feathers.

Conrad removed his chef's hat, and the men solemnly placed the wreath of victory on his head.

Conrad thanked them and then said that a toast was in order: "To Heavy!" he cried, standing up. "To Heavy, a truly great eater! And a great drinker! For Heavy had eaten before he challenged me, while I was working all day without eating anything. And that hardly makes for an even contest. If it had been the other way around, if Heavy had been doing the cooking and I the shooting—who knows what the outcome would have been. Heavy might be toasting me!"

All the men cheered at this.

Heavy smiled at Conrad, very appreciative, and tried to join in the toast. But he couldn't swallow any more beer. Someone laughed and said that if Heavy had done the cooking, the men would probably be shooting him now instead of toasting him.

After that all the men drank a toast to Conrad.

Conrad adjusted his red crown and then picked up the remains of his last bird.

The men suddenly fell silent. Incredulous, they watched him as he carefully detached one of the legs.

"Eggy!" Conrad called. "I need some more beer. And Harold—those birds must be done by now . . . Bring both trays. I'm hungry!"

II

XI

Mrs. Hill was perched on Conrad's stool, sipping a cup of broth, as was now her custom when she came into the kitchen to chat with him.

The relationship had grown steadily less formal, and sometimes Mrs. Hill sat in the kitchen for hours discussing matters and problems appertaining to the domain of food and domestic management. Maxfield resented this, and the first half-dozen times that he discovered Mrs. Hill in the kitchen talking to Conrad he sought to remain on some pretext, but Mrs. Hill had got rid of him, sending him on a duty to another part of the house, or with a message for Mrs. Wigton. Mrs. Wigton too felt she was being supplanted in Mrs. Hill's counsels, though there was little she could do about it, since she wasn't even allowed in the kitchen.

". . . Daphne is coming this Wednesday with Mr. and Mrs. Vale," Mrs. Hill said, taking a sip of her broth. "She rarely leaves the house, poor girl, but her parents have raved so about your cooking, and they insist that she come. —You know, Conrad, after you fixed Brogg's specialty for them Mrs. Vale hasn't said one good word about him. She's even said she would like to send him over to take lessons from you."

"I'm sure he'd appreciate that," Conrad commented, "from what I've heard about Brogg." He also had a cup of broth in his hand, though it wasn't the same kind.

". . . and when I told Mrs. Vale that I'd lost some weight since I've been eating your cooking—though I've actually been eating more, and everything that I want to—why, she actually began to blame Brogg for Daphne's being so fat. I had to remind her that Daphne was overweight before they got Brogg; after all, Dr. Law had suggested that she look for another cook, and told her of someone who was very well thought of in Highlands. That's when Mrs. Vale hired Brogg—though I will admit Daphne's continued to put on weight since he's been cooking for them, and maybe even at a faster rate. Poor girl, she's so fat. If only . . ."

She trailed off with a sigh, and her expression became remote, as if she could just picture a thin Daphne in a wedding gown, Harold by her side—if only . . .

❧

". . . Maxfield is sick in bed. I'm going to fix the drinks tonight." Harold walked over to the stove. "It smells good; may I ask what it is?"

"It's casserole of pheasant—the ones you shot the other day."

"But those were for you, Conrad," Harold objected quietly. "There'll be more than enough for all. The dish is very rich."

Harold smiled and shook his head. Once or twice a week since red-bird night Harold had brought Conrad several brace of birds to prepare for himself: "Anyone who loves wild birds as much as you do, Conrad . . ." he would say.

And Conrad would take the birds: "Red-bird night revealed one of my weaknesses, Harold."

It had revealed more than that. Not only had Conrad proved that he could out-eat anyone and out-drink anyone, but also that he could cook red-birds better than anyone had ever cooked them before.

He had also proved himself to be a prodigious and incredibly fast worker. Later that Saturday night, when Harold and he had finally got back to the Hill kitchen, Harold admitted he was on the verge of exhaustion, though he hadn't done one-twentieth of the work Conrad had.

"I don't know how you do it, Conrad," Harold said.

Conrad smiled. "Did you enjoy the work?" he asked.

Harold replied that he had enjoyed it very much. "I've also learned a lot. I never realized there was so much to cooking."

Conrad nodded understandingly. "You should look at some of my books on wild-bird cooking, and you'll see how many things we did wrong—necessarily, I might add: the facilities weren't ideal, and the number of short cuts we took—all to the detriment of the dish."

Harold looked a little surprised at this—whether at Conrad's invitation or at his strictures it was not possible to say —and after a slight hesitation replied that he couldn't imagine what else could have been done to the red-birds or how they could have been improved, but a few days later he referred to Conrad's remarks and Conrad again suggested that he take a look at the books.

"Do you want me to get them for you?" Conrad asked, as Harold looked a little shy, "or do you want to get them yourself?"

Harold replied that if Conrad didn't mind he would go up and look himself . . .

❧

"Oh, it has pictures!" Ester exclaimed happily.

At her request Conrad had given her the book on cat food.

After flipping through it and looking at all the pictures, she glanced at some of the suggested dishes. "Can you make any of these?"

Conrad said he could.

"Do you like kitties?"

Conrad replied that he used to have many.

"More than three?" Ester asked, incredulous.

"More than three," Conrad conceded.

"Oh, how marvelous! —I hate dogs," she added.

At last Ester pointed to a picture showing three kittens tumbling over themselves in eagerness to dispatch a dish of reddish-looking fish floating in green sauce.

"Next week," Conrad promised.

Conrad spent all of Sunday afternoon and evening at the Shepard's Inn drinking and listening to the gossip of the workingmen and servants who gathered there for the same purpose. Until quite recently most of these people would have gone to Ben's or the White Door or one of the other taverns. But word soon spread that whenever Conrad was at Shepard's, free hors-d'oeuvres and canapés were available. He prepared the tid-bits himself in the small kitchen in the rear of the inn. Also, Conrad was very liberal with his money; he would stand many rounds of beer and never ask for any in return. Word of this also spread, attracting customers.

There was a large table in a far corner, and this soon became known as Conrad's table. The customers who dropped in were made to feel free to pull up a chair and join him there, or leave him—as they chose.

Nell had been reduced to his willing but nervous slave. She did everything he said as fast as she could: if his beer was warm, she took it back; if it was flat, she took it back; if more plates were needed, she ran to the kitchen; if something was wanted from a shop, she screamed at Gimpy to fetch it; if Conrad left a message for someone, it was delivered; if someone left a package for Conrad, it was put on ice; if his table needed cleaning, she cleaned it, etc., etc. And it was always: "Yes, Mr. Conrad," or "No, Mr. Conrad," or "I'm sorry, Mr. Conrad."

Nell also related to Conrad any gossip which she thought he had missed and which might be of interest to him; and it was from her that he first heard that Ester Hill was seeing a boy in Highlands. "His family's none too good," Nell whispered, "and that's why Ester Hill is keeping it a secret." The boy's name was Lance Brown.

Conrad also learned from Nell that Brogg had been saying some very bad things about "that new cook at the Hills'."

And from some of the others Conrad heard that Mr. Hill had been proclaiming that he had the best cook this side of the City: "My fellow is really a magician with food."

Mr. Hill had added that he never felt better in his life and that he had actually taken off a little weight, though he was eating everything he wanted to.

XII

Most of the people who came to Shepard's had heard of Conrad's Tuesday dinners at the Prominence Inn. They knew that he reserved the private dining room for the occasion, that Charles cooked him special foods, that he ate all by himself and that he dressed formally. No one knew what to make of this, of course, but they opined that it surely must be expensive.

That was Maxfield's comment too.

He was fixing predinner drinks. It had been the first time in three days that he had felt well enough to perform that duty.

"I hear you have rather expensive tastes," he murmured.

Conrad, who was putting up some preserves, looked up from

the row of glistening jars that filled his worktable. "Meaning, I suppose, that I don't like to eat slop with pigs on my day off . . ."

Maxfield sniffed. "If you call eating with people of your own station—"

"Just fix the drinks," Conrad snapped; "that's what they're paying you for."

Maxfield spun around, livid.

"I'll thank you to remember I'm your superior," he spluttered. "I won't have you talk to me that way."

In his agitation he knocked over one of the glasses, spilling liquor on the floor.

Conrad laughed derisively. "What are you going to do about it? Sick butlers aren't at a premium. Neither are butlers who fake sickness. Either way you cut it, you're out. —Eggy! Clean up this mess—old Maxfield here is getting as clumsy as Betsy."

Maxfield started to reply, but as usual he suddenly felt too weak to fight Conrad. Besides, he was only just recovering from his sickness. He had been laid up for three days, supposedly with a severe stomach disorder. He took to his bed the afternoon Mrs. Hill told Conrad he should submit his accounts directly to her. Naturally, she had informed Maxfield of this change, and when Mrs. Wigton knocked timidly on the kitchen door and reported that Maxfield was very sick and would not be eating with her that night, Conrad retorted that Maxfield was merely sulking because he felt his authority had been undermined. "It's nothing to worry about, Mrs. Wigton. He'll be up and around once he gets used to it."

Mrs. Wigton said she didn't know what he was referring to.

"The accounts—that's all it is. I submit them directly to Mrs. Hill now. Maxfield has been cut out."

Mrs. Wigton was duly shocked and had left without saying a word.

". . . and Harold rather liked fixing the drinks," Conrad now continued to Maxfield. "Your services weren't missed in the least."

Maxfield replied quietly, "I shall speak to Mrs. Hill about this at the earliest opportunity. Your behavior is insupportable."

Conrad laughed again, holding a glass of clear red liquid up to the light. "Please do. Never bottle up your resentment. It will only give you ulcers—although you might have better luck if you speak to *Mr.* Hill; remember the accounts! And if you do speak to Mr. Hill, convey the cook's thanks for his raise in salary—it was more than double the contractual figure, and three months earlier than stipulated. Or hasn't anyone bothered to tell you?"

Conrad watched Maxfield's eyes widen in astonishment.

❧

When Daphne came with Mr. and Mrs. Vale, Conrad fixed her Brogg's speciality, which he had given her parents previously and over which they had raved so. This had been agreed on in advance with Mrs. Hill. "You can bring it out for her too, Conrad. The poor girl always seems to be depressed— a little extra fuss over her might raise her spirits." For the others he cooked something they had never had before.

The Vales were just an ordinary-looking couple, rather up in years and down in health, and it was hard to believe that the large blob of a girl sitting between Harold and Mrs. Hill was their daughter. She seemed to be twice their size, and without any signs of resemblance. That she was depressed, as Mrs. Hill had said, was obvious.

Conrad served her with decorous flamboyance and then withdrew, and when Betsy came back in the kitchen she said she was glad that Conrad had served Daphne Vale. "She looks like a pig. I don't like to serve her. And she never says anything—I never heard her say a word. She just sits. Sometimes she doesn't even eat."

Betsy continued to grumble as she came and went, bringing in and returning dishes.

". . . and she never laughs. She's disgusting . . . But I bet they don't talk about losing weight tonight, not with Daphne Vale sitting there. —Who is losing weight, and how much. That's all they talk about these days. And food—they don't talk about anything interesting any more. They just talk about food . . . They used to talk about things in town, and people. I used to hear about friends of mine who work for other families they know, and I used to tell them what I heard at table . . . And they used to talk about business, about cutting down trees and digging out stone—and Mr. Vale would talk about how he'd have to raise someone's rent, or who wasn't paying the rent on time . . . But they just talk about food now—and about who is losing weight. I couldn't care less . . ."

When Betsy came back after serving the dessert, she said that Mrs. Hill had asked her to inquire whether the dish Miss Vale had was "rich." Betsy snickered. "By that she means 'fattening.' "

Betsy delivered Conrad's answer, and returned looking a little surprised.

"I actually heard Miss Vale speak; she asked Mrs. Hill whether she might get the recipe from you since the dish was not rich."

Conrad asked whether Betsy had been sent to ask him for the recipe.

A slightly cunning smile turned up the corners of the maid's broad mouth. "I think Miss Vale expected Mrs. Hill to have me ask you for it; that's why she spoke up while I was there. But Mrs. Hill didn't do any such thing. 'I will discuss the matter with Conrad,' was all she would say."

"Very wise of her; find out whether Maxfield is well enough

to eat with Mrs. Wigton. —Eggy," he continued, turning to the
boy, who was clearing off the scraps from the plates, "see if
Rudolph is sober enough to eat."

"She enjoyed her dinner immensely," Mrs. Hill said. "She
even asked her mother whether they planned to come over
next Friday—so naturally, I invited her too, though the poor girl
should know that she's always welcome. After all, she stays
here for two months every winter. But I could see she would feel
better if I made the invitation specific. —She said she would
like to eat the same dinner all over," added Mrs. Hill as she
sipped a cup of coffee. She was sitting on Conrad's stool, leaning
back against the cupboard.

"Well, that's easy enough to arrange," Conrad said. "I don't
mean that I should send the recipe to Brogg. First of all, he
wouldn't appreciate it. Second, he wouldn't, and couldn't, do it
exactly the way it must be done; and third, I have little desire
to share the secret of the dish—no more than I imagine you
would care to have every cook in town capable of reproducing
the specialities of your table. There's something extremely
pleasant in knowing that no one outside your own dining room
is eating precisely what you are eating that evening. It unites
those at table in a unique, shared experience, which is also
quite delightful—don't you agree?"

Mrs. Hill smiled and said she quite agreed. She added that the
Vales, especially Mrs. Vale, had already asked her for the recipe
of practically every dish Conrad had prepared for them. "And
more than once. But I always say I will have to talk to you—
and then I never mention it again."

"And so," Conrad pursued, "why don't I make the dish here
and have it sent over to Miss Vale? That would solve everything."

"Send it over?" Mrs. Hill repeated. Obviously the possibility
had not occurred to her. "But could you do that?"

"Why not? We have plenty of containers."

"But wouldn't it get cold, for one thing?"

"Not if Rudolph went straight over and didn't stop for a drink on the way."

Mrs. Hill smiled. "His drinking is getting out of hand, isn't it?"

"Just a little."

Mrs. Hill began to get that dreamy look. "It's been a long time," she murmured, "since the Hill mansion sent dinners to the Vales, or vice versa. It was done in the past, so I've been told, when living and dining were in the grand manner. It might be nice to revive the custom."

❧

Mr. Hill always took lunch at the Prominence Inn, but one evening when Conrad was drinking at Shepard's he heard that Mr. Hill had become tired of the inn lunches because his cook had spoiled him. Now he demanded good food all the time. Indeed, he was thinking of giving up lunch altogether.

The next time Mrs. Hill came into the kitchen, Conrad said, "I could also have Mr. Hill's lunch sent to the mill every day. That way he would not have to distress himself with the efforts of the Prominence Inn."

Mrs. Hill beamed. "Conrad, you're a mind reader! Only this morning Benjamin said he would never go to the inn again for lunch. That's why he ate so many hors-d'oeuvres this evening: the poor man had starved himself from breakfast!"

When Conrad told Betsy to ask Mr. Hill if he would like lunch sent to him at the mill and if so at what time, the questions brought Mr. Hill to the kitchen.

Mr. Hill was profuse in his appreciation.

"I just can't bear to eat that food at the Prominence Inn

any more," he apologized. "You've ruined that place for me. Now I really know what good cooking is . . ."

He added, "And you know, Conrad, I'm losing a little weight . . ."

XIII

Conrad sent over the dish Daphne had liked so much to the Vale mansion. He gave Rudolph special instructions.

"Do not go to the kitchen door," Conrad told him. "There is a side door. Use it. Ask for Louise if she doesn't answer herself. She is Miss Vale's personal maid. Give these instructions to her." He handed Rudolph a folded sheet of paper. "Put it some place where you won't lose it. Tell Louise to take the carton to Miss Vale's room. It is her dinner, the one she requested from the Hills' cook. On no account is Louise to go to the kitchen with it—do you understand?"

Rudolph, standing stiffly in his bright-red livery, nodded dumbly.

"And do not linger on the way—not for a drink or for anything. I will find out, and if you do, I will put poison in your food and your skin will turn as red as your uniform and as hot as red coals—do you understand?"

Again Rudolph nodded.

"If you do as I tell you, I will make you a special dessert tonight, with black molasses—a whole plateful." Conrad demonstrated in the air the size of the plate he had in mind.

Rudolph grinned from ear to ear. Black molasses was his favorite sweet. "A whole plateful?" he repeated stupidly.

"Yes, a whole plateful. You didn't know there was that much black molasses in the entire world, did you?"

Rudolph shook his head, still grinning.

"Well, there is. Now get going."

Louise returned the plate and containers to Conrad personally. She wanted to tell him how much her mistress appreciated the dinner.

Conrad handed her a cup of coffee.

"Does Miss Vale have any other favorite dishes?"

"Oh, yes!" Louise rattled off several. "But I don't think they're good for her," she added sadly. "I think they're too rich."

"They won't be the way I fix them. —Will Miss Vale be home tomorrow night?"

Louise said she would be. "The poor girl doesn't go out very often. She won't even take walks with me any more. I try to encourage her but—well, Dr. Law says she's given up hope. And he says he can't help her if she won't help herself. But she wasn't that way before . . . oh, if only things were different, then maybe Harold Hill—."

"What about Brogg?" Conrad interrupted.

Louise's eyes suddenly narrowed. "What about him?"

"Does he know I sent that dish to her last night?"

"Certainly he does. I had the pleasure of telling him he needn't fix anything for my mistress, since he always complains about the extra work of having to send things up to her room."

"What did he say to that?"

The maid pursed her lips, and then her eyes began to fill with tears. "The man had the effrontery," she answered quietly, "to say it was about time my mistress stopped eating. But then I told him he was mistaken; that the cook at the Hill mansion had sent a special dish over to her, at Miss Vale's request. And you should have seen his face then!" The cloud lifted from Louise's face as quickly as it had come. She looked triumphant. "His face turned black and he started to utter some terrible oath, but I put my fingers in my ears and walked out of the kitchen."

Conrad laughed. "Good for you, Louise. You can tell your mistress she'll have something special tomorrow night. And she needn't worry about its being rich."

The little woman's eyes expressed her gratitude . . .

One morning Mr. Hill lingered over breakfast instead of repairing to the mill as soon as he'd finished.

"Breakfast was so good," he volunteered to Conrad, rather embarrassedly, "that I just didn't feel like rushing off. I just felt like enjoying another cup of coffee . . ."

Conrad replied that he could well understand it.

"Would you care to try one of these?" Conrad handed him a small, delicately shaped biscuit. It was semisweet and thinly glazed with fresh butter. There was a small tray of them on the sideboard. "They're especially fine with coffee around mid-morning. —I should like to prepare something special for tomorrow evening," he went on, giving Mr. Hill another biscuit, "but there's a slight problem: I would have to ask the

family not to have any drinks before dinner. The true flavor
of the dish is completely distorted by the slightest taint of
alcohol."

Mr. Hill shrugged and reached for another biscuit. "That's
a very small price to pay for a delicious meal," he allowed. "I've
often thought that alcohol dulls the palate anyway . . ."

⚜

That night Conrad went to the Shepard's Inn. He had taken
Rudolph with him, who in no time at all lay sodden in a corner,
his red livery collecting all the dirt from the floor.

During the course of the evening's drinking someone told him
that Brogg was looking for him.

Conrad laughed and bought the man a drink.

"He knows where to find me. That's no problem."

XIV

Conrad continued to send over two or three dinners a week to Daphne. He also sent a hot lunch to Mr. Hill every day at the mill, except when Mr. Hill lingered at home till noontime.

One morning Mrs. Hill came into the kitchen carrying the left-over breakfast things.

"You know," she began, "how much Mrs. Vale appreciates what you've been doing. Daphne is no longer so lethargic, and Mrs. Vale attributes this entirely to the change of food; when Daphne eats what Brogg cooks for her two days in a row, she gets depressed and refuses to leave her room."

Conrad answered that a change of diet was good for everyone.

Mrs. Hill agreed. "I have also told her that your kitchen account has shown no increase despite all the dishes you've sent to Daphne—and she replied that Brogg's has shown no decrease. She's quite annoyed with him."

Conrad said flatly that Brogg was robbing her.

"Oh, I'm sure he is. I've told Mrs. Vale too."

Conrad smiled.

"I'm just making some coffee for myself—would you care for a cup?"

Mrs. Hill said she would.

Conrad got out an extra cup and saucer.

And as he handed Mrs. Hill her coffee: "Why don't we get a scale?" he suggested, in a slightly offhand way. "I'm sure I can find one in Cobb at a very reasonable price. Everyone should know what his weight is, and whether it's remaining steady or going up or down. And when Miss Vale comes to stay with us—"

Mrs. Hill looked up from her coffee.

"Do you think it's possible for Daphne to lose some weight?"

"Why not? If she's fed properly."

He went on after a moment, "And with a scale here, she can weigh herself several times a week. If she sees she's losing she will get spirit and strive harder to lose still more. And if it appears that the entire household is weight-conscious, she won't feel like a fish out of water. It will be like joining in a family game—in which everyone weighs himself and records the figure. Each person can have his own weight chart. If he doesn't feel like revealing the figure he needn't. That's his business."

Mrs. Hill was intrigued. "Let me see, we had our first snow last week, on Saturday. Daphne's visit starts about a month after the first snow, when it's on the ground permanently—it's always been that way, since she was a child. The children always had so much fun playing in the snow together. She and Harold . . . And she will stay about two months . . . Conrad, do you think she can lose some weight in that time if she just eats your cooking? That's not a very long time . . ." Mrs. Hill seemed to think that considering Daphne's present size, it was no time at all.

"Certainly she can."

"But wouldn't it help," Mrs. Hill pursued after a moment, "if she began sooner?"

"Of course."

"What I mean, Conrad—suppose you sent dinner over to Daphne every night; then by the time she came here she would have some head start . . ."

Conrad smiled at the pleading look in Mrs. Hill's eyes.

"Just what I was thinking," he said. "And not only dinner, but everything else she eats. But we'll have to insist that Brogg prepare nothing for her. He may, at the most, warm up the things I send. And someone must watch him while he does that, preferably Mrs. Vale. Brogg might be able to intimidate Louise. But if Mrs. Vale is concerned about her daughter's weight she shouldn't be distressed by the extra duty."

Mrs. Hill looked extremely pleased.

XV

When the scale arrived, a practice weigh-in was held. Only Harold was absent, having already left for the mill. Ester joined in, but without any real interest. She did so only because her mother asked her. But she said that when the others were through, she was going to bring down each one of her kitties and weigh him.

"Do you want them to gain or lose?" Conrad asked her.

Ester replied that she wanted them to lose. She was very emphatic about it: "They're too fat. They can't even climb trees. And who ever heard of a kitty that couldn't climb a tree?"

The following Monday they had their first real weigh-in. Each person noted down his weight on a chart. Mrs. Hill, with Conrad's help, had drawn up charts for all of them. There was also one for Daphne and two for her parents.

When the ceremony was over and Conrad went back to the kitchen to put the finishing touches on dinner, he found Maxfield waiting for him, looking more bitter than ever.

"Hoping the dinner would burn?" Conrad inquired smoothly.

"In most households the cook's place is in the kitchen," Maxfield replied, "not with the family."

"I'm sure it is. But the scale is in the antechamber—care to know how much I weigh?" Conrad brandished his chart under Maxfield's nose. "Or the rest of the family?"

Maxfield sneered and backed away. "So now you're a member of the family? I'm sure they would like to know how you think of yourself."

Conrad ignored him, and set about getting dinner ready; this was the crucial time in the kitchen. Conrad moved fast, intently, like an enormous white praying mantis. Several times he had to push Maxfield out of the way. This he did unceremoniously, without a word, and each time the butler's face turned red and then white. At last Conrad pushed him aside so viciously that he tottered and almost fell to the floor. When he recovered his footing he stammered through trembling lips:

"I'm going to speak to Mr. Hill tonight and demand that he turn you out of this house. You're a—monster!"

Conrad laughed. "When you talk to him, tell him I too have a request: you're to stay out of my kitchen. If you come here again unbidden, I can't be responsible for your safety. You're a sick old man. You're liable to fall against the stove and burn yourself. Badly," he added, interrupting his chores for a moment to turn a black stare on Maxfield. "Is that clear? —Eggy!" he called, turning away from the alarmed butler. "Find Rudolph and tell him we're going drinking tonight."

Earlier in the evening the temperature had dropped, and by the time Conrad was ready to start for Shepard's it had started to snow. Rudolph walked beside him, struggling to maintain the rapid pace. He was carrying several jars of paté; he was tired and already half drunk, but the thought of more free drink was enough to entice him along. Besides, he wouldn't have dared to say no to Conrad's invitation. Harold's three dogs ran before them, frisking in the falling snow.

"Sobering up?" Conrad asked when they were about halfway there.

They walked on for several minutes before Rudolph answered that he was cold.

Conrad laughed heartily.

"Just cold, eh?" he exclaimed, slapping Rudolph on the back. "Very conservative response. Just symptoms, no diagnosis. You'd make someone an excellent patient."

When they got to Shepard's, Conrad greeted the assembled drinkers with a wave of his hand and a cheerful hello, and told Nell to fetch some crackers from the kitchen and to make some toast—he had brought along some good paté.

"It's brisk out tonight," he went on, slapping his hands together. "And it's not much warmer in here. Would anyone like some hot buttered rum?" It sounded as if the idea had just occurred to him. "Luckily I brought along plenty of butter," he laughed when a general smacking of lips and greedy growls of pleasure sounded down the bar. "Gimpy, get the rum bottle!"

It didn't take long for Shepard's to get warm, what with the hot drinks and the coal fire, which until Conrad came had been no more than a symbol of possible heat; at his command Nell had heaped it high with fresh coal. "And see that you keep it that way," he told her. "I'm used to a hot kitchen. If I were a butcher I might be used to a cold storeroom. But this isn't a place for storing meat. —Now, first we'll have some hot rum, and then we'll have some hot beer drinks . . . Gimpy, did you get the spices I asked for yesterday?"

Spirits rose, and the volume of talk and laughter increased with every fresh round of drinks. More people came, and by midnight the place was packed. Some of the newcomers reported that most of the other taverns were deserted. Shepard's had stolen all of the business. Even the White Door, they said, was empty; and when Conrad heard this he said to the group assembled at his table, "The White Door? Isn't that where Brogg holds court—hangs out, I mean?"

At the mention of Brogg, the men at the table suddenly became quiet.

Conrad smiled from one to the other. "Did I say a bad word?"

One of the men nodded. "Brogg's a bad word, all right. He's bad medicine."

Conrad raised his glass. "Here's to Brogg!" He drank off his beer. Two or three of the men sipped theirs, but that was all. "Nell!" Conrad shouted. "More drinks!"

When the drinks came, he said, "Well, I don't know if Brogg is bad medicine, but I do know he's a bad cook!" His voice rose. There was laughter and sarcasm in it. The men at the bar stopped their talking and turned around. The other tables grew silent.

"Brogg is a bad—wretched cook! For years now he has been cooking for the Vales. During that time the Vales have grown weak and sickly. Their daughter has blown up to the size of a house. Such is the effect of eating Brogg's food. But things are changing, and they will continue to change." He paused and tossed off his beer. Then he called for another round for the entire house. Murmurs of thanks greeted this.

Conrad stood up, thrusting his hands into his back pockets.

"Now," he continued, his tall black figure dominating the room, "Brogg no longer cooks for Daphne Vale. I cook for her.

Has he told you this? I send over every meal to her, because she refuses to eat his cooking. She says Brogg can't cook. He can't even cook his own so-called specialties. I cook all of these specialties for her, and I cook them better. Daphne Vale says Brogg's food makes her sick—I'm sure it does—and he has been forbidden to cook for her any more. All Brogg does now for Daphne Vale is warm up the food I send over. I have reduced the great Brogg to a mere warmer-upper—a warmer-uppper of the food Conrad cooks!"

Murmurs of surprise rippled down the bar and over the tables.

"Moreover, the Hills no longer eat at the Vales'. They can't stand Brogg's cooking. A week ago I sent some game over to the Vales' for Brogg to cook when the Hills dined there. But Brogg ruined it and the Hills said, 'Never again.' They said the birds were inedible. They said Brogg had done no more with the birds than render them warm and soft—that was what he called cooking! Warm and soft!"

Some of the people began to repeat the words "warm and soft," and others mouthed "warmer-upper" . . .

"And Mr. and Mrs. Vale," Conrad pursued, "used to eat at the Hill mansion once a week. Now they eat there twice a week— they would eat there every night if they were invited! They think Brogg is killing them with his food. And they're right. If I cooked for them I could put years on their lives. And I could make Daphne Vale thin—I *will* make Daphne Vale thin, very thin, because she shall only eat my food from now on. Brogg is out!

"Let me tell you this," Conrad concluded, raising his hand in the air and clenching his fist; "Brogg can't boil water! And if he asks who said so, tell him I said so: Brogg can't boil water!"

There were many loud cheers, and someone proposed a toast to Conrad. Then all the men began talking among themselves, discussing what Conrad had just said.

Paul was sitting at Conrad's table. He was on more familiar terms with Conrad than anyone else in Cobb, and when Conrad sat down he was looking very unhappy; he whispered that Brogg was sure to hear what Conrad had just said about him.

"I mean for him to," Conrad laughed.

Paul shook his head. "Brogg is vicious," he muttered. "He's big and he's vicious."

"I know; everyone is afraid of him. —Tell me more, Paul, tell me more . . ."

XVI

Rud Brogg was a huge bulky man, strong as a bull and, especially when he was drinking, far meaner. He inspired fear in all the other domestics and work people.

He usually came into Cobb on Wednesday night, and more often than not he would get into a fight, or bully someone into cowering submission. He was not liked. When he talked, everyone listened. His coarse jokes were always laughed at.

Conrad rarely came into town on Wednesday, and so the two of them had never laid eyes on each other.

As happens in the world of domestics, word spread quickly of the scene Monday night at the Shepard's Inn, and reached

Brogg's ear, and when Brogg dropped in at the White Door for his accustomed drinks, he was obviously in a violent temper. Men who drifted over to Shepard's from the White Door reported what Brogg was saying.

Conrad sat at his table in the corner and drank by himself.

It was cold that night. He had arrived late and the few customers there were surprised to see him. Nell was too, and she hastened to build up the fire. But that did little good and Conrad kept his heavy black coat wrapped around him.

Nell told him what Brogg was saying: "He is raving, they tell me. He says he is going to bone you like a chicken. He says he will cut you up like a side of beef. He says he will butcher you like a hog . . ."

Conrad sneered. "Don't you wish he would, Nell?"

Nell quickly denied the accusation.

"Sure you do, Nell. You don't like being my slave, even if it is good for business."

Again Nell objected, trying to look offended.

"You'd better deny it," Conrald told her coldly, "otherwise I'll start going to another tavern and you'll begin starving to death again. —Charlie!" he called to one of the men at the bar. "Come over here! —Nell, bring us two beers, quick!"

When Charlie, a balding, stoop-shouldered man, sat down, Conrad asked him to confirm what Nell had reported. Charlie looked nervous. He didn't want to get involved in the feud between Conrad and Brogg, but he admitted that every word Nell had said was true. "Brogg is after you, Conrad."

Conrad laughed. "Good for him!"

"You shouldn't be laughing, Conrad," Charlie muttered, shaking his head. "Brogg is a very good knife fighter. I've seen him . . ."

"Most cooks are," Conrad shrugged. "After all, they have knives in their hands much of the day."

Conrad finished his beer and stood up.

"I'm going over to the White Door," he announced. "Anyone care to join me?"

✿

Conrad strode over to the White Door. The three dogs romped ahead of him. Several paces to the rear four or five men, frightened and excited, followed.

Inside, Brogg was sitting at a large oak table. He was alone.

As Conrad entered he heard himself being vilified loudly. Brogg was talking to everyone and no one.

Conrad stood inside the door for a few seconds, then walked over and pulled up a chair to the table and sat down facing Brogg.

Brogg had large heavy features. His eyes were small and piglike. One of his huge hands surrounded a stein of beer.

Only his eyes had moved when Conrad entered.

The customers at the bar backed away, and joined the men who had followed Conrad in and who remained standing at the door. The fat tavern-keeper—the man who had first told Conrad about the Prominence and the Hills and the Vales—started to say something, but before he got more than a word out Brogg hurled the stein of beer in his direction without even bothering to look around. "Shut up!" he shouted.

His voice was brutal, animal-gutteral.

A nasty smile began to curl Brogg's thick lips.

"I was just about to go looking for you," he growled. "You saved me the trouble."

"I got tired of waiting. —Something bothering you, Brogg? Do you have something to say? If you have, say it. If you haven't—get out."

Murmurs of astonishment rose from the group gathered around the door. Conrad's voice sent a chill down their spines:

it was flat, cold, without a trace of feeling, and his challenge to Brogg was as direct and unequivocal as any challenge could be. It could not be ignored or misunderstood, and the blood mounted slowly to Brogg's face. At the same time his hand moved stealthily toward his belt: "This will tell all I have to say."

From his belt he produced a heavy boning knife with a black handle. The blade was about eight inches long. Originally it had been about three-quarters of an inch wide at the base, but years of use and sharpening had narrowed it to about half that width. Under the bright overhead light its blade glittered with marks of recent sharpening.

Brogg held the knife up for a few minutes, as if to let Conrad examine it. Neither man took his eyes off the other. Then Brogg laid it on the table midway between them, with the point facing Conrad. With his right hand—the same hand with which he had drawn the knife—he turned the knife a quarter circle. He did this very slowly, his beady eyes all the while exuding hate. The knife then rested with its point out to Brogg's left and its cutting edge facing him. He then slowly placed both hands on the table in front of him, the handle of the knife about four inches in front of his right hand.

Conrad placed his hands on the table, his left hand about the same distance from the knife handle as Brogg's right hand.

For several seconds the two men just stared at each other. From the way the knife was lying Brogg had an obvious advantage—assuming he was right-handed and wanted to use the knife in a certain way. But if he was left-handed, then it was equal between them—assuming Conrad was right-handed and wanted to use a downward thrust. But Brogg had withdrawn the knife with his right hand, which indicated . . .

Like lightning Conrad grabbed the knife with his right hand and plunged it with great force into the back of Brogg's left hand, pinioning it to the table, while Conrad himself was half catapulted to his feet, so great was the force of his downward thrust.

A loud gasp of astonishment arose from the men at the door.

Conrad sat down and folded his arms, while Brogg stared in stupid wonder at the knife sticking through his hand—and at the blood beginning to run around the blade and ooze over his hand onto the table. Three red rivulets started slowly toward his lap . . .

Slowly, as if he might hurt himself, Brogg's right hand touched the knife handle, and then closed around it. He seemed to have forgotten Conrad's presence completely. Gingerly, very gingerly, he began to pull at the knife handle. Beads of sweat formed on his brow. Now the red rivulets cascaded silently into his lap—

The witnesses gathered silently around the table. Not a word was spoken.

The moisture from Brogg's brow dropped onto the table, mixing with his blood, while in the hushed silence he pulled with all his might at the knife handle.

And then there was a sound: the sound of blood dripping on the floor—

Silently Brogg continued to tug at the knife handle. The knuckles of his right hand turned white with the strain. Any prizing movement would slice or tear the flesh further. He had to pull the knife straight up—

And then there was another sound: Brogg had begun to whimper.

Tears started from his eyes, and the fingers of his right hand slowly, jerkily, like a robot's, let go of the knife handle.

"I can't get it out!" he cried, almost inaudibly, his eyes fixed on the knife handle. "I can't get it out—"

Slowly he raised his frightened eyes to the circle of faces. His gaze passed from face to face, including Conrad's, whom he did not seem to distinguish from the other witnesses. "I can't get it out," he repeated. A note of hysteria crept into his voice.

He looked back at the knife handle—and at the confluence of the three rivulets at the edge of the table.

The sound of his dripping blood had changed: it was no longer dripping onto a hard floor; it was dripping into a pool . . .

"And I'm bleeding—" he whimpered, looking up at the faces again. "I'm bleeding—"

XVII

"Let someone else try," Conrad suggested coldly. "Perhaps they're stronger than you are, Brogg."

"Yes—let someone else try," Brogg agreed quickly, hope suddenly flashing in his eyes.

"Who wants to try . . . why don't *you* try?" Conrad indicated a fairly strong-looking man, who had been at the bar when Conrad came in.

"Yes, Ed, you try, you try . . ." Brogg exclaimed, almost happy through his tears—rather like a dog licking the hand that frees it from the trap.

"Try it!" Conrad demanded harshly when Ed seemed to hold back.

The man stepped forward and warily grasped the knife handle.

"Careful, Ed, careful . . . pull straight up—straight up—" Brogg directed in a weak voice, his tear-stained face now white and dripping with sweat. "Don't move it to the side . . . you'll cut me—you'll cut me if you move it to the side, Ed—"

But Ed muttered that he couldn't move it at all, and backed away from the table.

"Who else wants to try?"

Someone suggested that Curly try.

"Yes—you try, Curly," Brogg said eagerly.

Curly was the fat tavern-keeper. But as he grabbed the knife handle a wave of nausea suddenly swept over him, and he quickly left the table.

"Who's next?"

Someone—a little man—stepped forward. "I have small hands," he mumbled by way of an excuse. He grabbed the handle with both hands and tugged—

"Next?" Conrad called as the little man shook his head and backed off.

No one came forward.

"How about you?" Conrad asked a stocky, expressionless workman.

The man declined with a shrug. "Brogg's the strongest one in here. If he can't pull it out, no one can."

Brogg, listening intently, started to smile in silly agreement, but then suddenly bethought himself: "Sam, I'm left-handed . . . I'm left-handed. That's why I can't do it. You try . . . you try, Sam. You're strong—after me you're the strongest . . ." Hope again shone in the pinioned man's eyes.

"If you say so, Brogg, I'll try."

Sam stepped forward; he spat in his hands and rubbed them together. He planted his feet solidly. A look of determination came in his eyes, just as if he were essaying a feat of strength for a carnival prize.

He pulled with all his might. After several seconds he quit pulling and tried to jerk it out. He tried several hard tugs before he gave up. "No use," he muttered. "It can't be budged."

Brogg, who had been watching Sam's efforts with great hope, broke down completely at these words. "Please, please—someone pull it out . . . someone pull it out," he blubbered in a piteous voice. "Please—I'm bleeding—and it hurts . . . it hurts— Do something . . . please do something—Men, for God's sake—"

The group clustered around the table looked at each other. They obviously didn't know what to do. Two or three of the men looked at Brogg with some sympathy, but not too much. After all, he was the local bully, and they felt he was only getting what he had had coming to him for a long time.

Conrad, still sitting with his arms crossed, seemed to be the director of the scene but not one of the actors: having created the situation, no further contribution was expected from him. But when at last he cleared his throat all eyes turned to him.

"There is only one way, Brogg," he said quietly. "Only one way."

"Yes, yes—" Brogg exclaimed eagerly. But he obviously did not comprehend.

"Only one way," Conrad repeated.

For a moment Brogg continued to look dumbly at him—and then his eyes lit up with understanding. "Yes—yes, of course! Why didn't I think of it? You can pull it out! Of course—you can pull it out! You stuck it in, so you can pull it out!" Brogg began to laugh hysterically while he kept repeating: "You stuck it in, so you can pull it out!"

Conrad said nothing, but with great deliberation he reached

into the folds of his black coat and withdrew a broad, gleaming meat cleaver, and held it before Brogg's eyes. Not a sound greeted the appearance of this unexpected instrument. Even Brogg's blood seemed to have stopped dripping.

"I'm going to cut off your hand, Brogg. That's the only solution."

Brogg's mouth fell open. He started to protest, but instead a low scream escaped from the bottom of his throat.

***

Conrad drew the meat cleaver across Brogg's left wrist. A thin line of blood followed its path.

He drew the cleaver again across Brogg's wrist, this time below the wrist knuckle. "I think that will be better," he decided as he let the blade of the cleaver rest in the second cut.

Brogg's right hand moved slowly toward the cleaver, and touched it very gently. He seemed to think of trying to push it away. But there was obviously no hope of that. His will seemed to be completely broken. He let his hand rest against the side of the cleaver, as if with affection.

Pleadingly he raised his eyes to the group of witnesses—wouldn't someone help him? Wouldn't someone say something to Conrad on his behalf?

But he found no reassurance in the faces of the men observing his plight. Not only did everyone hate him—he had bullied them too long—but they were all afraid of Conrad. He was a kind of person they had never encountered before. He seemed to be without emotion, without anger. Perfectly calm and collected. He had pinioned Brogg to the table with no change of expression. And so firmly that no one could release him. And now he held a great, wicked-looking cleaver in his hand. No one felt like crossing Conrad. No one would take it upon himself to come between Conrad and his victim.

"Mercy . . . mercy—" Brogg whimpered. "Please have mercy—"

"No mercy. I'm going to free you."

Conrad pressed down harder on the cleaver. "Just one neat chop, right along this line." He raised the cleaver.

Brogg's eyes widened in momentary terror; then they rolled back and he fainted, his head falling forward on the table.

"Throw come cold beer on him," Conrad snapped.

Two or three hands obeyed immediately as Conrad jerked Brogg's head up by his hair. Beer streamed down his face and neck . . .

Brogg opened his eyes. For an instant he looked confused, then the horror of his situation returned to him.

"Try to pull the knife out again," Conrad told him. "I'll give you that chance."

Meekly Brogg did as Conrad told him. But he was too weak and broken in spirit, and he did little more than grasp the knife handle.

"That's enough. You're just wasting time. Better take your other hand away, or I'll cut that one off too."

In sick horror Brogg's eyes followed the slowly ascending arc of the cleaver while the witnessess backed silently away from the table.

Conrad held the cleaver poised for the stroke. Brogg's eyes, fixed on the cleaver, started to turn glassy . . .

One of the men coughed—

And then someone scraped his foot—

The cleaver still remained poised, about two feet above Brogg's pinioned hand: a horizontal furrow had begun to crease Conrad's brow. He looked somewhat thoughtful . . .

"Do you know, Brogg," he said quietly; "I've suddenly thought of something. Just this instant it has occurred to me that there might be an alternative."

He continued to hold the cleaver poised for the stroke.

Brogg's lips tried to form the word "What?", but neither his lips nor his tongue would do his bidding any more, and no sound came.

"Do you agree to the alternative?" Conrad demanded.

Brogg made his head nod.

"You still don't know what it is," Conrad reminded him. "I agree—"

Brogg's eyes showed no spark at the unexpected reprieve. It was as if he were beyond hope.

"After I tell you what it is," Conrad explained, "if you refuse I will immediately chop off your hand, six inches closer to your elbow—is that understood?"

Again Brogg nodded.

"Are you sure you understand?"

"Yes—"

"Very well." Conrad leaned forward and whispered in Brogg's ear. No one could hear what he said. Then he straightened up.

For a moment Brogg looked stunned. Then his expression became one of incredulity—

He began nodding wildly, even smiling. "Yes, yes!" he exclaimed. "Yes, yes!"

"You understand?"

Fresh tears began streaming from Brogg's eyes. Tears of relief.

"Yes, yes!" he repeated.

"Good. When?"

"When?" Brogg repeated. "Tomorrow . . . tonight—any time—tonight . . . tonight!" His voice rose out of control.

"Excellent. If you back out, Brogg," Conrad continued, "I will go over to your kitchen and cut off both your hands—do you understand?" He emphasized his intention by pressing the edge across Brogg's wrist again, drawing a third line of blood.

Brogg almost collapsed from fright, and blubbered and swore—

"Very well."

Conrad put the cleaver back in his belt, and grabbed the knife handle. With great effort he levered it forward, and blood poured from the fresh cut in Brogg's hand. Then, bracing himself against the table, he extracted the knife while Brogg let out a yelp of pain and grabbed his wounded hand, hugging it to his chest.

Someone threw him a rag and he began binding his bleeding hand.

"Now get out!" Conrad snapped.

Brogg pushed his chair back and stumbled to his feet. Broken, he staggered toward the door without looking around.

For a few seconds there wasn't a sound inside the White Door.

And then—

"Drinks for the house!" Conrad called. "Where's the innkeeper? And if anyone knows where Paul is, fetch him for me. I want to see him—Drinks!"

XVIII

Rud Brogg was seen no more in Cobb. He was replaced at the Vale mansion by Paul, on Conrad's recommendation. Mrs. Vale had come to Mrs. Hill in distress at the loss of her cook to ask if she knew of someone to replace him. Mrs. Hill had said she would speak to Conrad.

"But Paul is not a very good cook," Mrs. Hill objected when Conrad came up with his name. "I remember what the food was like when he was here."

Conrad agreed. "I know. But I will teach him to be a good cook. In six months he will be cooking better than Brogg ever dreamed of."

Conrad was as good as his word. He gave Paul constant ad-

vice and direction concerning the preparation of food, and provided him with numerous recipes. He also sent over special
ingredients for Paul—ingredients which Conrad prepared and
without which the dishes would have been only satisfactory and
not superior. Paul turned out to be a capable and ambitious
young man. He also acquired much of Conrad's dedication to
the culinary art, so that under Conrad's excellent tutelage he was
soon turning out dishes which earned him the Vales' appreciation
and praise.

III

XIX

"It's quite late and Daphne is already falling asleep—why doesn't she stay the night? We would be delighted to have her."

With this ritual invitation from Mrs. Hill, Daphne's annual house visit began.

The Hills and the Vales had finished eating dinner and were sitting around the fireplace chatting idly. And Daphne was indeed asleep, just as she had been as a small child when Mrs. Hill suggested for the first time that she spend the night. The night had become two weeks, and then months. Everyone enjoyed her presence, and the following year the visit was repeated— with Mrs. Hill issuing the invitation in the same manner, but as a joke, because the visit had been planned and Daphne had arrived that night with several boxes of clothes.

"Well, if you think she won't be a bother . . ." Mrs. Vale had smiled, going along with the joke.

"No bother at all. She can have the room next to Ester's."

It was the same room she had had on her first visit, and the one she was always to occupy subsequently. Of course it became known as "Daphne's room."

"Well, if you don't think she'll be a bother," Mrs. Vale smiled.

A few minutes later Mrs. Vale kissed her daughter good night, and Daphne went upstairs to "her" room.

❧

The biweekly weighing sessions, which had been instituted just before Daphne's annual visit began, continued after she had arrived and quickly became the most anticipated domestic event of the week. Mrs. Hill induced Daphne to participate in these—she could weigh herself in privacy, before or after the others. The girl was at first extremely reluctant, but after recording a lower figure on three consecutive weighings she began looking forward to Monday and Thursday evenings more than anyone else. And it was this fact (that she was steadily losing weight—an open secret in the household, though no one knew exactly what she weighed) that lent to the sessions their significance and excitement: if Daphne continued to lose weight— why, wasn't it possible that she would eventually make a bride for Harold Hill? And if the Hills and Vales intermarried—why, then the Prominence would once again become the ancestral home of the heirs and descendants of the family of Cobb.

"Isn't that wonderful, Conrad?" Mrs. Hill exclaimed one Thursday evening as she settled on his stool. "Daphne has lost another four pounds!"

Conrad agreed it was wonderful. "We'll have her in shape before anyone knows it. —And what about you?"

Mrs. Hill laughed. "Oh, I'm not important. But I lost another half-pound, or just about. And so did Benjamin. He's looking so much better!"

It was true too. Mr. Hill looked five years younger than when Conrad arrived: he was trim rather than bulky and his face was no longer florid.

"And feeling better too?" Conrad asked.

"Oh, yes, much better. —And you, Conrad, did you gain any weight this week?"

Conrad replied that he had put on another pound since Monday.

"That makes me very happy," Mrs. Hill smiled. "You must put on another forty or fifty pounds, maybe even more. You're a very big man . . ."

"Maybe even more," he agreed.

"And Mrs. Vale says she's so glad I included them when I made up the charts," continued Mrs. Hill. "She can't wait to tell Dr. Law—not just about Daphne losing weight, though that will really surprise him, since he had given up on her completely. He said there was no way in the world to make that girl lose weight. But then, he also said that Mr. and Mrs. Vale were just naturally in delicate health and . . ."

"They're gaining too, aren't they?"

"Oh, yes. And feeling much better."

Conrad said he was glad to hear that. "Paul must be carrying out my orders. —More broth?"

As Mrs. Hill took another cup of broth, Conrad told her that he had something to show her. "These just came from the City," he said, handing her two very expensive-looking brochures. The word CHINA was embossed on the cover of one, and on the other GLASS. "I thought you might be interested—they're from the best china and glass shops in the City, as I'm sure you recognize from the names."

Mrs. Hill took the brochures, and almost at once her eyes began to pop with delight and excitement at the handsome colored illustrations.

"They're beautiful! Absolutely beautiful! I had no idea there were such things . . ."

Conrad waited till she was quite carried away by the pictures of the china and glassware—indulging herself perhaps in dreams of possession—and then he said, "Well, you know we don't have a complete set of either in the house. Betsy's heavy hand has seen to that. I've spoken to Maxfield about it, but he's too old and broken in spirit and too lacking in taste to appreciate the importance of proper tableware. He said that as far as he was concerned the family could continue to eat off cracked dishes and unmatched sets. But excellent food, supreme dishes, demand more than mere receptacles. Superb settings—not just adequate —are required."

Mrs. Hill was listening to Conrad and looking at the illustrations at the same time.

"Maxfield is getting too old," she declared.

"And when I spoke to Mrs. Wigton," Conrad added, "she said Maxfield had already forbidden her to discuss the matter of tableware with me."

Mrs. Hill frowned. "Maxfield is becoming senile. I must speak to Benjamin about him. —Oh, look at this!" She pointed to an especially striking set of dishes. "Aren't they lovely?"

Conrad glanced at the dishes from where he was standing. "How many pieces?"

"Let me see—seventy-two."

"Well, at the rate Betsy would break them . . ."

Mrs. Hill continued to pore over the brochures.

Conrad got a few things ready for next morning's breakfast.

"Look at this!" Mrs. Hill exclaimed every few seconds.

"Yes—"

"Oh, Conrad!"

"Yes, that might do."

"Do you like this pattern?"

"Yes, very sensible. They're not too expensive either. And with the money we've saved on the kitchen accounts—"

"Conrad, don't worry about the money."

"Fine. The best is never cheap."

"Just look at this crystal!"

"Yes, that caught my eye before. —Don't forget your broth now," Conrad reminded her. "It's getting cold."

Mrs. Hill reached abstractedly for her cup of broth, and began sipping it without removing her eyes from the dazzling illustrations in the brochures.

"Let's pick out a few patterns," Conrad suggested, "and send for some samples. That is the only sure way to tell. Pictures have a way of lying."

Had Mrs. Hill been a child, she would have clapped her hands with delight.

Two hours later Conrad and Mrs. Hill said good night. The patterns and samples to be sent for had been agreed upon, and Conrad had promised to write for them.

XX

Harold had read Conrad's books on wild birds and then, very diffidently, he asked Conrad if he would teach him how to prepare grouse. Conrad said he would, but the matter wasn't mentioned again till one day Conrad said he was going to fix grouse for the family and reminded Harold of his request. Thus, Harold got his first formal cooking lesson.

Harold was extremely pleased. He asked many intelligent questions and did everything Conrad told him. Conrad was an excellent teacher, and in effect, Harold prepared the grouse while Conrad supervised.

During occasional respites from the actual work their talk

wandered to diverse subjects. They talked about Daphne losing weight, and about Ester gaining weight—the latter circumstance, though evident to all even before the scale had been installed, was never alluded to by Mrs. Hill. Perhaps it didn't disturb her, or perhaps she thought it would upset Conrad if she mentioned it, as if it were the sole black mark on his otherwise perfect record. Or so Conrad had thought. But Harold offered another interpretation.

"I suppose you know," he said, in a slightly confidential voice, "that Ester has a boy friend—Lance Brown. The rumors of it are all over Cobb."

Conrad said he had heard.

"Well, Mother has heard it too, and she and Ester had quite a row; Father doesn't know yet. But Mother can't do anything with Ester—she continues to see him. There's nothing really wrong with the boy. It's just that he has a bad reputation, and his family . . ."

"Yes, I've heard," Conrad helped him out.

Harold went on after a slight pause, "This may sound crazy, but I think Mother hopes that if Ester gets too fat—well, that Lance Brown will give her up. Rather," he explained in some embarrassment, "like Daphne's case . . ."

As Harold continued to look perturbed, Conrad told him he had better stir his sauce, and be sure to scrape the bottom of the pan very hard: "It's those little brown-black particles adhering to the bottom that really matter," he explained; "without them the sauce would be nothing."

Harold stirred vigorously.

"And how is your weight coming?" Conrad asked idly as he went about the business of preparing Daphne's dinner, which was always different from the family's.

"If I ate lunch," Harold said, "I would probably gain."

Conrad laughed. "Harold, that's not the reason you don't eat lunch. You can't stand the food at the Prominence Inn any more, and you think I have enough work as it is without fixing a special lunch for you."

Harold looked up from his stirring and nodded.

Conrad laughed again. "But you know, Harold, Charles is really a very good cook. It's the people he cooks for—they're used to eating that kind of food."

"I don't know, Conrad. Some of that stuff Charles turns out for lunch—"

"Yes, but that's lunch for everybody else. He must cook that way for them. But he doesn't cook that way for me. —Listen, to prove my point: would you care to have dinner there with me when Charles cooks something special? Then you will see what I mean."

Harold looked at Conrad in wonderment. "Do you mean it?"

"Yes, of course."

"But I've heard the way you dine," Harold demurred. "They say course after course . . . unheard-of dishes . . . and all sorts of wines and liqueurs—with extraordinary china and silver you've had specially sent from the City . . ."

"They exaggerate. I have a friend there who has allowed me their use."

"And all the waiters hovering around you . . ."

"Only four."

"And they say the food alone costs a fortune —"

Conrad laughed. "Not true, Harold. You've heard rumors, just rumors—it's really all rather simple. But the food is good."

It was Harold's turn to laugh. "I'm still not convinced! When I hear how you eat there, I always tell myself that you do all the cooking yourself and then have Charles and the waiters serve you your own food. Or perhaps you let Charles warm up a few things. Anyway, Conrad, my palate isn't refined enough for such dining. I fear the food would be wasted on me."

"Nonsense. Your palate is quite subtle. And if it's not discriminating enough, there's only one way to improve it—taste."

Harold still protested that the food would be wasted on him, but after a little more persuasion he at last agreed, and the Tuesday following the next was decided upon.

It was probably Harold's appreciation of Conrad's confidence that prompted him, later the same evening, to invite Conrad for a visit to the Prominence. The two of them were doing a little cleaning up in the kitchen—Harold's grouse dinner had been a great success; he had, however, made Conrad promise to tell no one of his hand in it—and the talk had turned to kitchens: Conrad said some kitchens were pleasant to cook in, and others impossible, for various reasons. Some were too big, others too cramped. Some too light, others too dark. Others were poorly ventilated. Still others were laid out abominably: sinks here, stoves there, racks there, coolers here, cupboards there, workplaces there—all in one perverse composition.

Harold was listening attentively, a very pleased look on his face because of his success with the grouse.

"I've only been in one other kitchen besides this one," Harold said; "the one at the Prominence. It's enormous; I would never have imagined such a kitchen existed. And it's so elaborate—I suppose by any standards."

Conrad stopped what he was doing, and his large black eyes were suddenly bright with interest. Perhaps it was this sudden attention which caused Harold to break off.

"I don't suppose I should be telling *you* about kitchens," he apologized awkwardly. "You know more about them than I ever will . . ."

"On the contrary," Conrad assured him. "Tell me more. Tell me all about it." And he sat down on his stool and folded his arms, prepared to listen.

But Harold just grew more confused. "I really don't know how to describe it. It's extremely big, and full of all sorts of copper things—sinks, drainboards, pots and pans . . ." He broke off, and as Conrad waited for him to resume his description, a light began to shine in Harold's sensitive eyes. "I tell you what, Conrad!" he exclaimed. "I have an idea: why don't we go up there? Rather than have me describe it—which I can't do anyway—I'll take you up there for a visit. You can look at the kitchen and see for yourself. And while we're there I'll show you the entire place. I'm sure you'd like it—it's something right out of the past. It's unbelievable . . . there are rooms enough for hundreds of people—which probably explains the size of the kitchen: it's big enough to prepare food for a small army— even when I think of the stories I've read about the way the old landed gentry used to eat . . . hundreds of years ago . . ."

But even while Harold was talking so enthusiastically, Conrad began shaking his head. Possibly Harold at first thought Conrad was shaking his head in disbelief, but as Conrad continued the negative movements, Harold at last realized his words were not getting a favorable reception.

"No," Conrad told him, "I do not want to pay a visit to the Prominence. No visit, Harold . . ."

❦

The night was cold and clear. The snow was about a foot deep.

Conrad walked around the side of the house, the three dogs following him.

In the cold clear moonlight the Prominence rose commandingly from the plateau. It was a thing out of the past.

No, he repeated to himself as he stared at the looming Prominence, he did not wish to pay a visit to its kitchen.

Never, he thought. He shivered in the cold, and with one last look at the ancient structure he turned toward his room.

XXI

Late one night Conrad wrote a letter to a gentleman in the City—a well-known gentleman; one of the persons, in fact, who had given him a character reference for his present employment—a man whom Mr. Hill, when he saw the signature, had said he himself would feel honored to know. Well, he was going to be given his chance, because Conrad was writing to confirm a date he had suggested for dinner in Cobb, at the Prominence Inn. Naturally the day would be Tuesday. Harold would be there and so would Mr. Hill, as Harold's guest. Harold had invited him. It had come about in this way:

Harold dined with Conrad on the Tuesday they had appointed, and he was so overwhelmed by the setting in the private dining room and by the transformation of Conrad that he scarcely said a word throughout the entire dinner.

Conrad—or "Mr. Conrad," as Charles and the waiters called him—did all the talking, from the moment Harold walked into the dining room and received a welcome from what was evidently a king sitting at the head of a long, candle-lit table.

Checking a movement to bow, Harold sat down.

The food was excellent. Conrad explained the history, so far as it was known, of all the dishes: their antiquity, their place of origin, their creators and whom they were created for. He also had what was evidently a bottomless fund of anecdotes concerning the dishes: the failures, the successes, the reactions they inspired in people first savoring them. Dish after dish came, and Conrad would ask Harold if he was interested in learning any of their secrets. Harold's eyes lit up with eagerness greater than mere curiosity, and Conrad proceeded to detail for him the exact preparations and techniques involved. Moreover, he said that if Harold was interested, he could teach him how to make every dish they were having.

Harold stopped eating for a moment. "If I'm interested . . . " he murmured, as if his interest could but be taken for granted. "Of course I'm interested . . ."

Conrad laughed pleasantly, and said well then, he would be able to prepare a dinner like that before he knew it—and the young man murmured his thanks . . .

Harold ate until he was stuffed, but good as the dishes were he could not possibly eat all that was set before him, and he watched with unbelieving eyes while Conrad ate and ate, possibly four times the amount he had consumed, yet with no appearance of becoming the least bit satiated.

And when they had at last finished, Conrad said, "I won't invite you at this moment to dine with me next week, Harold. I fear you are too full, and you probably feel certain you will never eat again. That feeling will pass, of course. When it does, then I will issue the invitation."

Harold dined the following Tuesday with Conrad, and every Tuesday of the next month. During the week he would spend as much time in the kitchen as possible, watching Conrad and listening to him explain various culinary procedures. Whenever Conrad entrusted him to perform some minor operation, he bent all of his effort and attention to it. He was also reading more of Conrad's books, carrying them surreptitiously to the mill in the morning.

One Tuesday night, when they had finished eating and were sipping their final liqueur, Conrad—following a momentary lull in his flow of talk—casually mentioned he was thinking of having a friend down from the City to dine with them.

"He's a close friend of mine," he continued; "we have shared many excellent repasts. Mr. Bayard is a fine gourmet and a charming companion at the dinner table."

Harold, who was just raising the needle-stemmed liqueur glass to his lips, re-placed it with great care on the table.

"*The* Mr. Bayard?" he asked quietly and with great respect.

"Yes. We've known each other a very long time; in fact, he gave me a character reference when I came to Cobb. He thought it very amusing that *he* should be giving *me* a character reference!" Conrad laughed gayly at this. "Perhaps your father would like to meet Mr. Bayard?"

Harold was still unable to adjust to the familiar interjection of such a great name into the conversation, much less to the assertion that such a figure would soon descend into their midst for a dinner, and it was several seconds before he was able to nod a mute assent.

"Well, if you think he would," Conrad went on; "invite him.

He will be your guest. You and I will be sort of joint hosts for the occasion; I will confirm the date."

Harold was still reacting inwardly to Conrad's mention of his friend and could do little more than express his thanks; but the next morning he came into the kitchen before he left for the mill and told Conrad of the effect his offer had had on his father.

"Father wouldn't believe me!" he laughed. "He thought I was just joking. And then, after I had convinced him I was serious, he began to raise objections: he wasn't used to dining with such people. He was just a simple man, born and raised in Cobb, and wouldn't know how to behave in the presence of such a figure from the City . . . and more of the same. But I told him not to worry . . . that it would be a very pleasant and simple dinner. Nothing more—" Harold laughed mischievously. "Conrad, I wouldn't dare tell him what it will really be like. If he knew how elaborate your dining room is . . . he thinks it's just the way it was when he was last there, years ago—"

Before Harold left the kitchen he took three cook books out of one of the cupboards. "I'm comparing them as I go along," he said, "just as you told me to."

That morning was an awkward time for Mr. Hill. He lingered over breakfast so long—drinking extra cups of coffee and nibbling at the little tid-bits Conrad sent Betsy in with every so often—that it was soon too near the lunch hour to leave for the mill. No doubt he had stayed on deliberately: he would have to say something to Conrad sooner or later, and he might just as well get it over with. His opportunity came at lunch, when Conrad decided to serve, along with Betsy.

Mr. and Mrs. Hill and Daphne were seated in a semicircle at the table. Ester wasn't there.

Conrad set Daphne's special lunch in front of her, acknowledging with a curt nod the look of heartfelt appreciation in the

stout girl's eyes. He then turned to Mr. Hill, who kept his eyes
fixed on his plate, saying nothing—which was unusual. When he
stayed for lunch Mr. Hill would make some kind of joke about
his presence, usually attributing it to the seductive quality of
Conrad's coffee and tid-bits. "The kitchen has become an al-
chemist's shop," he would laugh.

Conrad quietly gave the name of the soup they were having,
and left.

When he returned the second time Mr. Hill still could not
meet his eyes. Nor the third—Mr. Hill stared either straight
before him or down at his plate.

But on Conrad's fourth trip Mr. Hill, doubtless fortified in
mind, body and soul by the delicious food he'd been eating,
cleared his throat and said, "Harold tells me you're having a
friend down from the City . . ."

Conrad looked down at Mr. Hill.

"Yes. Mr. Bayard. We're having dinner."

"Yes. Harold said that was the gentleman."

"If you would care to meet him . . ."

Mr. Hill waited in vain for Conrad to complete his sentence.

"Harold said . . ." Mr. Hill began, and then hesitated, still
looking at Conrad, as if he were expecting him to repeat the
invitation. But Conrad merely continued to look down at him
in silence. If Mr. Hill had anything to say he would have to say
it, and in the momentary silence the invitation to dine with
Mr. Bayard and Conrad took on a different complexion: Mr. Hill
would have to ask if he might join them.

"I should like to meet him," Mr. Hill said at last, in a very
friendly way.

Conrad nodded curtly.

"Good. Then we shall dine together."

That afternoon, when Conrad went shopping, he gave the provisioner of canned goods a long list of things he wanted ordered
from the City. Then he met Paul at Shepard's and told him to

find the fishermen: "The Vales are coming over, and I want Harold to practice a sauce."

❧

Harold was sitting in a chair, an open cook book in his lap.

Conrad was lying stretched out on his bed. His tall chef's hat was still on, half crushed beneath his head.

"Now listen carefully," Conrad began. "It's all in the blending . . ."

For half an hour Conrad explained the preparation of the sauce while Harold listened with an aspect of complete absorption, his brow slightly furrowed and his gaze completely steady. It was an expression which no one else had ever seen him assume, and which would have surprised him had he been able to observe it. But it only came over his face when Conrad was talking about cooking, when he was doing something in the kitchen to assist Conrad, and when he was reading the cook books. On all other occasions he wore the same dreamy, sensitive expression which Conrad had noted upon first seeing him.

Harold asked a few questions after Conrad had finished, and then inquired as to what time Conrad thought he should begin.

"Right after lunch, no later. That way you will have time for three attempts, should something go wrong. Can you get away from the mill?"

"Yes, I'll just leave. Father will have to stay. He won't like it, I know; I suppose you've noticed that he doesn't stay at the mill any more on Saturday afternoons?"

Conrad said he was aware of that: "Nor does he ever go on Sundays."

"No, he doesn't. —It's funny," Harold continued after a moment, his usual dreamy expression replacing his look of studied concentration, "very funny about Father. He used to love the mill. He used to love going there—not that he really had to. It's so well organized that he has little more to do than watch it in operation. But it gave him something to do, something to build his day around. But he has been changing— just within the last few months. He no longer likes to go there. And sometimes he doesn't get there until the afternoon. And then when he does get there I have the feeling that he would like to leave and come back here. I haven't talked to him about it, but I think he would rather stay home all the time. You've noticed that he never goes out any more in the evening. And he used to dine out at least twice a week, either at the Vales' or at the Prominence Inn . . ." Harold trailed off in an abstracted way.

From the way he was talking he did not seem worried about his father's health or state of mind.

"I'm sure he's in excellent health," Conrad said, reading Harold's thoughts.

"Oh, I'm sure he is too," Harold agreed. "It's just strange that —I wonder why the dogs are kicking up such a fuss?"

The sound of furious barking had suddenly erupted in the night.

XXII

"It's Rudolph. He's drunk again and has fallen into the snow at the edge of the road; he can never make it all the way back from Cobb. It happens every night."

Harold looked mildly surprised but said nothing.

"I'll have to help him," Conrad said, getting up. "Only the alarum of the dogs saves him from freezing to death. —We're going to have to get rid of him. He's as worthless as Maxfield, or almost. Maxfield has been in bed for a week now. And of course," he added with a contemptuous snort, "there's that gem of a maid—Betsy."

"Has he?" Harold murmured vaguely. "I *thought* I hadn't seen him."

The two of them went downstairs into the moon-lit night.

Conrad told Harold he would get Rudolph—Harold hadn't his coat with him. "I shall see you tomorrow after lunch."

The white moon was resting on the far parapet of the Prominence, bathing the ancient structure in light, and Conrad stood contemplating it for a long time, ignoring the loud snores of the crumpled figure at his feet.

At last a thin smile relieved the fixity of Conrad's expression. A few minutes later he began kicking Rudolph to his feet.

❧

When Mrs. Hill came into the kitchen, Betsy was still there stacking up some of the dishes. Mrs. Hill dismissed her. "That girl," she said impatiently, "makes me nervous just watching her. I'm surprised we have any dishes left. But when we get our new sets . . . Now, isn't there something I can do here?"

Conrad told her there was nothing more to do except put the glasses away, and he indicated the cupboard where they belonged.

The two of them rapidly got the kitchen in order, Mrs. Hill humming to herself the while. When she had finished she settled on Conrad's stool, and he told her that he would have their broth ready in a jiffy.

"Is my broth the same as yours?" Mrs. Hill asked, as she did practically every night, and Conrad replied, as he always did, that there was little difference: "Mine is a tick more highly seasoned."

"I must try yours sometime," Mrs. Hill smiled.

"Yes. —And Daphne, how was her weight tonight?"

Mrs. Hill told him, and then began adding up the number of pounds Daphne had lost since her arrival.

"She won't put them all back on, will she, Conrad?"

"Never," he assured her.

"And she will continue to lose?"

"Yes, provided she eats what I feed her."

"Oh, she will—I know she will!" Mrs. Hill exclaimed. "She loves your food and she says she always eats until she's full—and she can't understand that. And she claims she never has that hungry feeling any more. —She's such a sweet girl." As Mrs. Hill said that a dreamy expression came over her face—it was easy to see where Harold got his from. "And Daphne is such a pretty girl," she continued after a moment; "I just couldn't help thinking as I looked at her next to Harold at dinner tonight how nice they looked side by side—he so fair and blond, like all the Hills, and Daphne with her dark beauty. I can't help thinking . . ."

Conrad sipped his broth. "She will look nice in white," he said, very matter-of-factly.

"Yes, she will," Mrs. Hill murmured, and then lapsed into silence, the better to savor the image.

At last Mrs. Hill returned from the future: "She is supposed to go home this Sunday—do you think there is any chance of something happening if she leaves?"

"Do you mean, will she gain weight?"

"Yes—will you be able to send all of her food over? Or will it be safe for her to eat Paul's cooking—I mean, provided you tell him how to cook for her?"

Conrad riveted Mrs. Hill's eyes into focus—they had a tendency to flutter—and replied in no uncertain terms:

"It would be better if she stayed. Much better . . . much, much better. No matter what one tells another cook it is not possible to guarantee the dish. So far, judging by the weight Mr. and Mrs. Vale are putting on, Paul has followed my instructions to the letter. But I cannot be certain he will continue. And as for resuming my catering and delivery service—that was an expedient at best. The results have been far superior since she came here. I am sure you agree. Living here is good for her. She should stay. On no score do I recommend that Daphne leave the Hill mansion until everything is settled—I mean everything. There is no reason to incur a risk which is unnecessary, and returning to the Vale mansion is not necessary."

Mrs. Hill understood Conrad perfectly, and as he talked she nodded in agreement, her lips tightening: it was the marriage that mattered, and that was all.

She finished her broth before she replied, "I shall speak to Eva Vale tomorrow and insist that Daphne stay. I shall tell her that you refuse to be responsible . . ."

Conrad nodded.

And as Mrs. Hill started to leave: "You know," she said, "our samples of china should arrive this Saturday . . ."

Though it was quite late Conrad went into Cobb. There were no customers at Shepard's, and standing at the bar he drank a few steins of beer. Nell had a little gossip for him.

"I hear," she said, "that Ester Hill sees Lance Brown practically every day now. They say her parents don't know about it and that she has to sneak away from the Hill mansion."

"People exaggerate," Conrad reminded her. "What else do you hear?"

Nell replied that that was all people said, except that Ester seemed to be getting very heavy. "They say she's suddenly begun putting on weight—rather like young Miss Vale a few years ago when just all of a sudden she started to gain and didn't stop until she was as big as a house."

Conrad finished his beer. "Miss Vale is only the size of a small cottage now. —When Charles comes in, tell him I'll see him to-morrow, either here or in the kitchen. —Do you have my clothes in order for Tuesday?"

❦

When the samples of china and glass arrived, Mrs. Hill told everyone that as soon as lunch was over they would have to vacate the dining room: there was to be no lingering over extra cups of coffee, and second and third desserts—she and Conrad wanted to be alone. They had something to discuss. She also told Mrs. Wigton she wanted all of the table-cloths and napkins available.

Conrad unpacked the samples and set them on the dining-room table. Betsy brought in the table linen and stacked it on one side of the table, as she was told. When she saw the samples of glass and china, her mouth literally fell open; obviously she had never before seen anything so magnificent and expensive-looking. But she recovered quickly, commenting: "Oh, my! Aren't we getting fancy now!"

The superciliousness of this remark irritated Mrs. Hill. "That will do, Betsy. You may leave. Please see that you do not return until you're called. We do not wish to be interrupted."

"Yes, ma'am," Betsy curtsied, casting a final look at the glittering samples.

The process of selection then began: deciding what they liked best, and matching glass with plate, linen with glass and linen with china—and all with the décor of the dining room. "And this book will help us," Conrad said. "It contains numerous illustrations of some of the most sumptuous tables ever set."

Mrs. Hill let out a gasp of astonishment at the sight of the first illustration of truly luxurious dining.

"Do you think we'll be able to teach Betsy how to set a table like that?" Conrad asked. "I wonder—I really wonder . . ."

Mrs. Hill's murmured answer was inaudible.

XXIII

Mrs. Hill reported that Daphne would stay for another month.

Conrad replied that a month would not be quite sufficient: "It will take six weeks. By that time she will weigh between one-twenty and one twenty-five."

"Are you sure, Conrad?" Mrs. Hill smiled.

"Yes. You may order clothes on that assumption."

They had agreed on the china and glass to be ordered and Mr. Hill had been called in to concur. His eyes popped when he saw the samples.

"Such china seems too fine to use," he murmured.

"Well, we are going to use it," Mrs. Hill retorted. —"Now look at this." She held open the book of table settings. "This is the way we are going to set our table when the new china and glass arrive—isn't it, Conrad?"

Mr. Hill stared at the beautifully colored illustration. "Do people really eat at tables like that?"

"Well, of course they do! And we will too. We're going to teach Betsy how to set a table like this—aren't we, Conrad?"

"We're going to try."

Mrs. Hill laughed. "*Try* is right! That girl! I might end up having to do it myself. With you helping me, Benjamin."

"We might all have to do it," Conrad conceded.

※

"Gentlemen," Conrad was saying to the three men facing him, "we will all participate. The dictum 'too many cooks spoil the dish' must give way to the requirements of specialization. Besides, there will only be one in charge. I have brought the marinades." He indicated two earthenware pots sitting on the table. "Charles, you will start on the meat dish tonight . . ."

They were sitting in the Shepard's Inn at the corner table.

"Paul," Conrad continued, "will do the soup and pastries. Harold will do the sauce for the birds—he has been working on it diligently for the past week—do you think you can do it, Harold?"

"If you have confidence in me, Conrad . . ."

"All the confidence in the world. —Charles will do the vegetables. I will prepare all the other sauces . . . The earlier we begin the better. I will come about ten. Harold . . . ?"

Harold said he would leave the mansion with Conrad: "Father will simply have to go to the mill that morning."

XXIV

Monday evening the temperature started to drop, and light snow-flakes began to fall. It continued to snow throughout the night, and Tuesday dawned biting cold and with a veritable blizzard in progress. All the old snow had been covered during the night with a thick layer of blazing white; it was already more than four inches deep on the steps to Conrad's room. As he came down, kicking off the snow on his way, he thought what a perfect day he had chosen for the special dinner: outside, miserable cold, everything obliterated by layers and clouds of white, and inside, a great hospitable fire, a great table laden with delicious food, warming wines . . . And to be in perfect health, with a gargantuan appetite, a refined taste—what could be better?

In the kitchen he found Eggy and Rudolph shivering and trying to get warm; they had apparently just come in from the shed. Harold was also there, waiting for him. "I made some coffee for you," he said with a slightly embarrassed smile. "I hope it's good . . ."

"Thank you, Harold," Conrad said, "thank you very much. That will save us some time."

Conrad, Charles, Paul and Harold worked very hard that day in the Prominence Inn kitchen. Nothing went wrong, and by seven in the evening Conrad and Harold were free to leave and dress for dinner.

Mr. Bayard had arrived a few hours earlier and was resting in the bridal suite on the top floor.

❀

Conrad was standing by the large open fire at the rear of the private dining room when Harold and Mr. Hill came in. As Harold had said, Mr. Hill still pictured the dining room as it had looked when he used to visit it, and at the sight of the changes which Conrad had wrought—the heavy, lush drapes, the paintings on the walls, the great silver candelabra—Mr. Hill stopped dead in his tracks: he couldn't believe his eyes. Indeed, he couldn't have been more surprised had he discovered himself suddenly and mysteriously transported to the most exclusive dining club in the City.

Harold gently led him over to the fireplace, and to the tall saturnine figure in formal evening attire standing beside it. Instinctively, as if to assure himself of the figure's good will, Mr. Hill held out his hand.

"Rennie Bayard will be along in a moment," Conrad said easily. "Would you care for some sherry?"

One of the four waiters, standing like statues around the table, moved, and brought Mr. Hill a small glass of pale amber-colored liquid.

"Rennie said he is of good appetite," Conrad smiled. "I am too . . . and you?"

Mr. Hill replied that he hoped he could do justice to the dinner.

Conrad answered that he was sure he would.

"But my tastes aren't as refined as yours, Conrad," Mr. Hill murmured in apology.

"It's only a matter of training," Conrad explained. "One must only concentrate on the taste he is experiencing while he has the food in his mouth—ah, here comes Rennie now."

Mr. Hill and Harold turned around as the gentleman in evening clothes approached them. The word "rotund" might be the first to enter one's mind at the sight of Mr. Bayard, but "well-fed" would be more apt, and as Conrad did the introductions, Mr. Bayard's smile revealed large, solid white teeth—teeth which somehow seemed just made for eating with.

Mr. Bayard closed his eyes and sniffed the air, like a deer.

"The bouquet is a most rare one these days, most rare indeed," he murmured. "Where did you get the sherry, Connie? Unearth a cache of it in Cobb?"

"If I told you, there soon wouldn't be any left."

Mr. Bayard chuckled. "True, Connie, too true. You had best keep your secret."

Mr. Hill said nothing the while, and when he tasted his sherry again it was with a new and deep reverence.

"Can you hold your own with Connie when it comes to eating, Mr. Hill?"

Mr. Hill's eyes flickered up from the floor to the face of the man he was so honored to meet, and he hesitated, smiling. He wasn't quite sure what the question meant.

"If you can," went on Mr. Bayard, "you're in a very select circle."

Mr. Hill smiled at Conrad and at Mr. Bayard.

"I'm afraid I don't know much about food," he murmured quietly. And as both Conrad and Mr. Bayard continued to look at him as if they were expecting something more: "I'm afraid I'm what I've heard called a gourmand and not a gourmet—why, until Conrad came here, I didn't even know what good food was. I just ate what was put in front of me . . ."

Mr. Hill began to perspire under the strain of his long speech, and as he spoke Mr. Bayard arched an eyebrow in surprise.

"Really?" He clearly found Mr. Hill's demurrer hard to believe. "Well, be that as it may," he smiled as Mr. Hill started to repeat his disclaimer of gourmet pretenses; "under Connie's expert tutelage it won't be long before all that's changed. He—and I speak as one who has observed—has educated the most recalcitrant of palates. Connie—remember when you introduced Monte Springhorn to cuisine in contrast to food? Monte," continued Mr. Bayard to Mr. Hill, "with all his money, had never even seen, much less tasted, a truffle. He was a meat-and-potatoes man. And one night Connie here . . ."

Mr. Bayard proceeded to tell Mr. Hill and Harold—who was standing beside his father, smiling and diffident—an amusing story concerning the aforesaid person's initial contact with truffles and how he had carefully extracted them from beneath the poached chicken's skin and pushed them to one side of his plate, thinking they were dried and burnt clots of blood, etc.

But Mr. Hill heard scarcely a word of the story: the mention of Monte Springhorn's name had stupified him. He was the wealthiest person in the City and one of the most politically powerful. The discovery that Conrad was on close terms with him shattered whatever remaining notion Mr. Hill had that Conrad was still, after all, only his cook . . .

". . . Excellent sauce," pronounced the great gentleman. "Absolutely superb."

Conrad nodded toward Harold.

"Did you make the sauce, young man?"

Mr. Bayard congratulated Harold and added, jokingly, that he would like to hire him as a cook.

Conrad laughed and said, in the same vein, that Harold was not for hire. "You people from the City must find your own cooks."

Harold looked extremely pleased.

Mr. Bayard and Conrad did all of the talking, mostly about food and previous dinners they had eaten—some in each other's company, and some not. When a dinner was discussed where one of them had not been present, the party were all duly named, then the cooks who had prepared the dinner, and all of the courses served. The scene thus set, the actual food was discussed, and anything else of interest that had occurred.

Mr. Hill listened to the conversation in open awe. So many great names were thumped against his brain that by the time the fifth course arrived he could not have felt more insignificant had a campaign of belittlement been deliberately waged against him. And as he grew smaller and smaller, Conrad, sitting at the head of the table—so tall and regal, in perfect evening dress— seemed to grow larger, and larger . . .

Mr. Hill was also getting drunk.

With the greatest care Mr. Hill picked up each of the glasses ringing his plate and set them back several inches. He then pushed his plate into the space he'd created, and put his head where his plate had been.

Conrad told Harold to finish what he was eating, and then

Harold and two of the waiters got Mr. Hill to his feet and out of the dining room.

"Do you know," Mr. Bayard smiled when the door had closed, "your friend looks just like those pictures of old-time butlers gracing the stately homes . . ."

"Doesn't he though!" Conrad agreed with a laugh. "And the more weight he loses, the more he resembles one."

"Extraordinary! Too bad one can't find them any more . . . But as you were saying . . ."

Harold returned, smiling, and apologized for the interruption.

"Think nothing of it," Mr. Bayard assured him. "It happens to the best."

"I think I know why he drank so much wine," Harold continued to Conrad. "He got quite a shock today."

Conrad looked at Harold inquiringly.

"He found out that Ester is engaged to marry Lance Brown."

IV

XXV

By the time Daphne's six additional weeks were up she weighed an even one hundred and twenty pounds, and looked happy and beautiful. Her engagement to Harold Hill had been announced the week before. The marriage was to take place in June.

And as for the other engagement . . .

On Conrad's advice Lance Brown was made welcome at the Hill mansion.

He was not a very intelligent lad. He had a low forehead and a rather weak mouth. What Ester saw in him would be hard to discover. But what he saw in her was clear: money. If he were able to marry into the Hill family he would be set for life.

Yet his experience of rich living was anything but to his liking. Every time he ate the Hills' food he got sick, very sick.

And every time he came over it must have seemed to him as if Ester was gaining another pound. Under his eyes, as it were. Because she was always seated right across from him.

Indeed, was he going to take a house for his wife? What would people say?

❦

After Daphne's engagement to Harold Hill had been announced, it was decided that Daphne should extend her visit still longer. Or more precisely, that was Conrad's position. "I won't say she'll have to remain here till June," he told Mrs. Hill, "but she will have to stay at least another month, and preferably a month and a half."

"By the way," he said after a moment, "are Mr. and Mrs. Vale still gaining weight? I assume they are."

"Oh, yes," Mrs. Hill assured him. "They're almost plump now—or they *seem* plump after being so thin all these years. And they say they never felt better . . ."

XXVI

"... so he says she's getting too fat—he blames you—and he's going to take her away."

Conrad smiled at the news. "The boy shows spirit. —And what will he do with her when he has her?"

Nell replied that Lance still lived with his parents and he would probably just take her home with him.

Conrad laughed. "Nell, you're out of touch. The Browns can't afford Ester. She'd eat them out of house and home in less than a month."

Nell thought that over for a moment. "Maybe he expects the Hills to give him some money."

"Maybe."

"Well, anyway, that's his problem. I don't know what he's going to do with her. But don't say I didn't warn you."

Conrad raised his stein in acknowledgment.

Later that week Ester made one of her infrequent appearances in the kitchen. It was just after breakfast.

Conrad quit what he was doing and stood up.

"And to what do I owe this pleasure?" he inquired brightly, offering Ester his stool.

The girl just stood there for a moment, and then she leaned back against the stool—she couldn't possibly have hitched herself onto it. For several seconds she said nothing.

"Will you do me a favor?" she asked finally. "I want a favor."

"Oh, yes, by all means," Conrad answered quickly. "Just name it." Conrad waited patiently.

"Next Tuesday morning," Ester began haltingly, "I am going away. I am going to leave here before my mother and father get up."

Conrad nodded. "I see. I see. You are going to leave very early. Just after dawn."

He paused, but Ester made no objection to the time.

"Very good, very good," he went on. "I understand. You are going to run away. You are going to elope."

Ester showed no surprise. After a few seconds she blinked her eyes in what was evidently assent.

"Excellent, excellent. You are going to run away with Lance Brown. Fine. And now, how may I be of assistance to you?" Conrad crossed his arms and waited.

"I shall miss breakfast," Ester declared, rather forcibly.

"Yes, that you will."

Ester began to look a little animated.

"And I shall miss lunch."

Conrad shrugged. "It depends where you're going."

"To Highlands. We have to row across Blue Lake—that's where I'm meeting him. It will take a long time. We won't get to Highlands till late."

"Yes, very late," Conrad agreed. "You might even miss dinner. That's possible."

"Yes."

Ester's momentary animation faded. Indeed, she began to look miserable.

"Well?" Conrad prompted. "What is it you want of me?"

Ester slowly leaned forward and said, in a voice just above a whisper, "Please—please pack a picnic basket for me—a big picnic basket . . ." There was a pleading note in her voice, a note almost of fear.

Conrad smiled at the girl benignly.

"Ester," he said quietly; "that's no problem. Of course I shall pack a picnic basket for you. I would have done so even if you hadn't asked—I know what such journeys are like."

He paused, and then added, smiling, "I shall pack you the biggest picnic basket you ever saw."

It took a second or two for these words to soak in. Then Ester's broad cheeks rippled, and she smiled. And as her smile grew broader she gave a little chuckle.

When next Tuesday morning came, Conrad roused Rudolph from a drunken sleep and dragged him into the kitchen, where he stood rubbing his eyes, not knowing what he was doing.

"Here, drink this," Conrad said, thrusting a hot cup of coffee into Rudolph's hands. "You'll need it to sustain yourself—we have a rendezvous at Blue Lake."

Sleepily Rudolph obeyed, nearly scalding himself on the coffee.

Ester was leaning back against Conrad's stool. She also looked half asleep. On the floor beside her was a drawstring bag from which the head of a cat protruded, Queen Bee III, licking lazily at a saucer of milk. Next to the bag was a small valise.

Conrad poured himself a cup of coffee and then went over to the open door.

"Ah, it's going to be a beautiful morning!" he declared. "A beautiful morning! Indeed, a spring day in winter; and down in the lowland, a summer day! A summer day, with no snow—just bright, fresh, appetizing air!"

Conrad breathed in the cool morning air.

"Yes, a perfect morning—a perfect morning for a little walk, for a little jaunt down to the lake. Indeed, it looks like a perfect day for a picnic!"

He laughed and thumped himself on the chest. "Yes, a perfect day! Are we ready? Rudolph, you carry that." He pointed to a very large knapsack stuffed to bulging. "It's heavy. I'll help you strap it on your back."

Rudolph bent over and Conrad hoisted the huge knapsack onto his shoulders.

"There. Now, can you straighten up?"

Rudolph was able to unbend to about a three-quarters position.

"Marvelous! Marvelous! You'll be able to hobble along just fine like that!" Conrad gave Rudolph a reassuring slap on the back, which sent him reeling toward the back door. "Careful, don't stumble!"

The three of them started out, Conrad carrying the valise and Ester with Queen Bee III.

"We'll go this way," Conrad said, turning off the road. "The footing's a bit tricky on occasion, but as a ramble it can't be beaten. There are stiles and creeks and marshes and little up-and-down ways—nature at its best with just a small assist from man.

"Come, Ester," Conrad continued, taking her hand and helping her over a minor declivity; "just watch where you put your feet. We don't want any sprained ankles at the outset. Nothing to mar a beautiful day . . . After this we go down a little hill."

Esther plodded along behind him, with Rudolph struggling in the rear.

At the foot of the hill Conrad stopped and filled his lungs with the fresh morning air. "Ah, there's nothing like a brisk morning walk to stimulate the appetite. Absolutely nothing to compare. I recommend it for everyone.

"That's a good girl, you're doing just fine," Conrad congratulated Ester as she stepped over a branch in the path. "Now mind those thorns. We don't want you to tear your dress—it's such a pretty dress too, with such lovely pink flowers. I'm sure Lance will be pleased."

Carefully Ester negotiated the hazard . . .

"Wonderful! Wonderful! I can see that you were born to the outdoors!"

Meadow followed hill and hill meadow, until finally all the small hills were behind them.

"See, I told you we'd leave the snow behind!" Conrad laughed happily as he led the way toward a shadowy marsh. "Just step where I step," he advised the girl. "I don't want you to get stuck. Better still, take my hand."

And, as hand in hand they entered the marsh: "Oh, a' picnicking we'll go!—A' picnicking we'll go!—Hi-hi-hi-ho—A' picnicking we'll go!"

Conrad had a ringing bass voice.

❧

As they penetrated the marsh, day was left behind. The overarching trees with their matting of leaves and vines and dead branches made a veritable tunnel. Only where the tunnel had fallen in was the sun able to strike directly to the path. For the rest, there was but a dim twilight.

The path itself—if it could be called that—was a treacherous one. It wound around trunks of trees and low-growing thickets. Occasionally it led into a positively impenetrable tangle that had to be skirted, and then the path picked up once more on the other side. Or again, it would all but disappear among muddy sink-holes and pools of stagnant marsh water. Sunken and half-rotted logs formed makeshift bridges. And sometimes there were only clumps of semisolid marsh sod to use as stepping stones —where a slight misstep could plunge one into water and mire of unknown depth.

Conrad moved along the path like a hummingbird. He was in front of Ester, behind her, and all around her. Unerringly he guided her along the way, sometimes leading her by the hand, other times pushing her gently from behind. Where there were only logs to cross on, he put his arms around her and steadied her as she stolidly planted one foot in front of the other. When she was safely across, he would laugh and congratulate her and pat her on the cheek.

He was also constantly running back to Rudolph.

"I can't let anything happen to my bearer," he would laugh. "He's got all the food!"

And all the while Conrad was singing . . .

At last they reached a patch of more or less solid ground and Conrad said they would sit down and have a little rest.

Rudolph lay down and immediately fell asleep.

But Ester—Ester just stood there and marveled at Conrad.

"Come now," Conrad said kindly; "you must have a little rest. We still have some distance to go and you're not used to walking—you want to be fresh for Lance, don't you?"

"Lance . . . ?"

And she continued to stare at Conrad as he took her by the

hand and led her over to a log. "Rest here," he said quietly. "I'll get you something to nibble on."

They rested for half an hour. Conrad opened the knapsack and busied himself with some of its contents.

All the while he sang. And every so often he would smile at Ester and hand her a different kind of bon-bon.

And Ester's gaze was constantly fixed upon him. . .

Conrad paced the journey well. He allowed two more rest stops, a half-hour each, and then, when they were just about ready for a third, the marsh gave way to the open shore of Blue Lake.

"Ah, here we are!" Conrad declared. "Feel the good sand beneath your feet! The inlet will be just up there."

But Ester held back, as if she needed rest before continuing. "Come," Conrad coaxed her, taking her hand. "It's not much farther. Then you can rest as long as you like."

For a moment Ester just looked at him, not moving. Then dutifully she gave way, and hand in hand they trudged along the sand.

". . . and doesn't the air smell good," Conrad chatted, "so clean, so fresh . . ."

The inlet was small and shallow, and ringed by a narrow strip of pure white sand. Half pulled up on it was a small rowboat.

Lance Brown was sitting in the sand on the other side of the boat, facing the direction of the road. He didn't hear Conrad and Ester approach.

"Here we are!" Conrad boomed down at him.

The young man leaped straight up in the air.

"Don't be frightened," Conrad laughed. "I've brought Ester."

It took Lance some time to recover his wits, and when he was at last able to talk he remarked peevishly to Ester that she was late.

"Yes," Conrad admitted, "we are a little late. We took the scenic route—but it was worth it, wasn't it, Ester?"

Ester said nothing.

Rudolph came up beside them, half doubled over with the knapsack.

Conrad unbuckled the straps and hoisted the knapsack from Rudolph's back. "Yes, it certainly is heavy," he said to a relieved Rudolph.

He put the knapsack in the boat, and the stern promptly sank and came to rest on the bottom.

Lance, his little eyes blinking furiously, was berating Ester for being late. He reminded her that someone was supposed to meet them on the other side of the lake and take them to Highlands. "They won't wait," he complained. "We'll have to walk all the way. We won't get there till way after dark."

Conrad interrupted him. "Lance, look—you're going to have to row very carefully."

Lance glanced from Conrad to the boat. "What's in the knapsack?" he asked.

"Why, what do you think? A wedding present."

Dumbly Lance repeated Conrad's words, and then pushed at the boat. It didn't give an inch. "But what's in the knapsack?"

It was Ester who answered: "Food."

"Well told! Well told!" Conrad exclaimed. "Food!"

But Lance just frowned. "Thank you, but we can't take it. The boat will sink with all that food, and Ester."

Conrad laughed and went into the water, pulling Rudolph with him. Together they dragged the boat into deeper water until it was floating. "There! See, it floats."

Lance began to look very unhappy. "Just barely. And it won't float at all with Ester and me in it. It will sink."

"Ha! Nothing ventured nothing gained!" Conrad declared, wringing the water from his trousers legs.

Lance, however, remained reluctant. But he was also afraid to look at Conrad . . .

Conrad slapped the youth hard on the back. "If you don't get any wind you'll be all right. Just take it slow and careful. Your chances will be excellent. Come on, get in. As you said, you're already late."

Conrad propelled Lance into the water. Lance waded to the boat and started to get in. But when he saw how low it sank he changed his mind and hurried back to shore.

"Ester," he whined, "if we try to go with that knapsack we'll drown. It will just take a little cross-breeze. Tell—tell Mr. Conrad we can't accept his wedding present. We'll have to leave it behind. Tell him . . ."

There was fear in Lance Brown's voice—fear of offending Conrad and fear of drowning.

But Ester refused to help him; she probably didn't even hear him: she was looking fixedly at Conrad.

Lance continued to plead with her, and insisted they had to leave immediately. "Just tell Mr. Conrad we can't take his wedding present . . ."

At last Ester seemed to come to some decision, and she took a step toward Conrad.

"Let's have a picnic," she said. "Right here—now."

At these words Conrad gave vent to a burst of uproarious laughter, which lasted several seconds. Then he gave Ester a kiss on both cheeks. "What a perfectly ingenious suggestion! Perfectly ingenious! —Rudolph, pull the boat in! We're going to have a picnic—did you hear that! The three of us are going to have a beautiful beach picnic!"

Conrad turned on Lance. "Move! You're standing where I'm going to lay the picnic cloth."

Lance Brown began to tremble at Conrad's sudden change of voice and expression. It was impossible to misinterpret its menace.

The young man stumbled toward the water's edge.

"Get in the boat," Conrad ordered. "Rudolph, give me the knapsack. Help Lance—push him out . . . Row, Lance—row, row . . ."

Conrad's laughter followed Lance Brown out of the inlet.

"Wave good-by! There he goes—wave . . ."

But Ester wasn't listening. She was sitting on the sand. Queen Bee III, released from her confinement, was playing happily in the sand. "We're going to have a picnic, kitty," Ester murmured. "We're going to have a picnic . . ."

The next morning when Conrad served breakfast he gave Ester a conspiratorial wink.

XXVII

Conrad and Mr. and Mrs. Hill were eagerly looking forward to the arrival of the new dinnerware; indeed, from the time Mr. Bayard had hand-carried the order to the shop in the City, that was practically all the three of them talked about. That Conrad and Mrs. Hill were excited was only natural. But that Mr. Hill was so interested can only be explained by the profound effect the dinner with Mr. Bayard had had upon him.

The morning after that evening, Mr. Hill did not go to work. He lingered over the breakfast table till it was time for lunch. After lunch he retreated to his den and did not reappear till about an hour before dinner, when he came into the kitchen and said hello to Conrad.

Harold was in the kitchen, working on that evening's dessert. Father and son smiled at each other, and Conrad told Mr. Hill what Harold was doing. Mr. Hill was very interested and watched Harold for several minutes. While he was looking over his son's shoulder, Betsy came in and reported to Conrad that Maxfield was still too ill to come down and fix drinks.

Conrad turned to Harold.

"You can let that go now," he said; "fix the drinks instead."

Harold started to wash his hands. Mr. Hill watched him for a second, then went over to him. "I'll fix the drinks, Harold. You finish what you're doing. —I know what your mother and Ester want, but what is it Daphne takes?"

"It's all in the cupboard there," Conrad said, indicating the door above the end of the worktable. "The rose and yellow bottles are Daphne's. Two parts of the rose to one of the other."

Mr. Hill quickly went to work, and Harold returned to the large tray of curiously shaped dough. "I hope it comes out all right," Harold smiled.

"It will," Conrad assured him.

Mr. Hill left with the drinks, and when he returned he asked if Conrad and Harold would care for something.

"Yes," Conrad answered. He gave Mr. Hill very specific instructions on how to fix two drinks for Harold and himself, and after Mr. Hill had made the drinks Conrad sat down on his stool and tasted one, licked his lips and pronounced it excellent. Mr. Hill smiled his appreciation for the encomium, murmuring that he had only followed directions.

The next evening Mr. Hill again made and served the drinks, and for the rest of the week—during which time he did not spend five hours at the mill, all told. Each evening Harold and Conrad took a half-hour off from their duties to savor their drinks —a different one each time. On Saturday night when the Vales were over for dinner, Mr. Hill prepared the drinks for all. Rudolph was in the kitchen that night and somehow got the idea into his head that he should serve the drinks Mr. Hill was preparing. But when he stepped forward to take the tray, Conrad ordered him to leave it alone and get back into the corner.

"You're too drunk to be of any use," Conrad told him. "You're of no more use than Maxfield, who's been lying in bed for the past week, sick or feigning sickness. We'd be better off without both of you."

Mr. Hill did not wait for Conrad to finish berating Rudolph but left with the tray of drinks.

"Rudolph will have to go," Conrad declared when Mr. Hill came back to ask Conrad what he and Harold wanted. "He's corrupting Eggy. Eggy never had a drink in his life till the other night. Rudolph threatened him and made him drink. That night I had to do the dinner dishes myself—Eggy was too drunk and sick to do anything. And Betsy—if I had waited for Betsy to do the dishes they'd still be dirty—at the rate she moves."

Mr. Hill listened to Conrad but answered nothing in return, which was the way it had been since the night of the dinner: he would listen to Conrad's remarks and nod, but no more. In fact, when Conrad had served the family breakfast that Saturday morning, Mr. Hill broke off his conversation with Mrs. Hill when Conrad appeared. He even stopped eating. Later that morning Mrs. Hill came into the kitchen and told Conrad what they had been talking about.

Mr. Hill was excited about the dinnerware, which was due to arrive the following Wednesday.

"He can't wait," Mrs. Hill said. "He's as excited as I am. —When do you think we should begin trying to teach Betsy the new table settings? We don't have much time, and knowing that girl's stupidity and stubbornness . . ."

Conrad said he wasn't sure, but he was afraid they would have to wait until the dishes arrived. He doubted whether Betsy would be able to learn from the illustrations in the book. "I don't believe she could be made to understand that the illustrations represent actual tables with china and glasses and silver on them. It would be a feat of abstraction beyond her. However, we'll talk about that later."

Later was that evening, after the Vales had left. The dinner had been elaborate, with course after course coming until the Vales were so stuffed they could scarcely move. Because of the dinner's timing complexities, Harold had remained in the kitchen helping Conrad, and had not joined the guests. He even served one of the courses—one he had prepared almost entirely by himself. If the Vales were surprised at the sight of the son of the house appearing with a large silver tray in his hand and a small cook's cap on his head, they contained their surprise and took their lead from Mr. and Mrs. Hill, who smiled approvingly at Harold and inquired whether he had made the particular dish he was bringing.

Conrad served the next course and came back to the kitchen with the silver tray which had borne Harold's effort:

"See, it's empty. Not a bite left on it."

Harold smiled at the empty tray.

"They must have liked it," he murmured.

"Of course!"

Harold looked very pleased.

The two of them worked steadily until at last Conrad said they were through and could relax and eat their own dinner.

"How do you feel?" he asked. "This is the first time you have worked all the way through a dinner."

"Tired," Harold admitted.

"Very understandable. But you'll get used to it."

"I think we used every pot and pan in the house."

Conrad started to reply that he was sure they had, when a screechy voice from the direction of the sink interjected: "And every dish too!"

Conrad turned around: Eggy never talked without being spoken to first.

"What did you say, Eggy?"

Eggy giggled, and then repeated his remark. "And I'll have to wash every one too!" His eyes rolled foolishly.

Conrad walked over and pulled Eggy off the stool by his ear. "You've been drinking. —Rudolph, of course."

Conrad propelled Eggy toward the back door. "Sleep it off. I'll wake you later. And you will wash every single dish, if you have to stay at the sink all night. You will get no food till you're all through."

XXVIII

But when Conrad roused Eggy a few hours later with a sharp kick in his rib cage, Eggy proved to be more drunk than when he'd been chased from the kitchen. He could barely stand, and his eyes would not stay open.

"Has Rudolph given you more to drink?" demanded Conrad. "If he has he's worked his last day here."

But Eggy was in no condition to understand the question.

Disgusted, Conrad threw Eggy back on the old mattress, covered him with a few blankets and left.

"Shall we wash the dishes ourselves?" Harold asked when Conrad told him that Eggy was still incapacitated.

"No. We'll leave them till the morning. Eggy will have to

work all day Sunday. It's as simple as that. —Go to bed, Harold. You look completely worn out."

Harold, stifling a yawn, admitted he was.

After Harold had left, Conrad sat on his stool.

In a few minutes Mrs. Hill came in; she always waited till she heard Harold go upstairs to bed.

"That was a delicious dinner," she smiled. "Everyone ate till he was stuffed. And the Vales! They're so plump and jolly now, and they eat more than anyone else. I've never seen such a change come over a couple. Before, they were pale and in delicate health, and afraid to eat anything but fish. But now they gobble down everything in sight, and always seem to be looking for more—"

"Eggy's drunk," Conrad interrupted. "Rudolph gave him liquor again. He was too drunk to do the washing-up."

Mrs. Hill frowned.

"I've sent Betsy to bed," Conrad went on after a moment. "She'd be at it all night, and then be of absolutely no use to-morrow. Harold was too tired to help. He worked very hard this evening."

Mrs. Hill pursed her lips: she had made a decision.

"Well, *I'm* not too tired." She started toward the pantry. "Are the aprons still kept in here?"

"Only Harold's."

Mrs. Hill found Harold's apron, wrapped it around her, tucked it in and made it very neat. "There!" she said. "It will do just fine. Now, I'll be back in a minute."

Conrad removed his apron and laid it on Eggy's stool by the sink.

Mrs. Hill returned shortly with a slightly embarrassed-looking Mr. Hill. "Benjamin is going to help," she announced.

Mr. Hill smiled but said nothing.

"It will help you sleep," Mrs. Hill went on; "a little exercise after a large meal never hurt anyone."

Mr. Hill made no objection. On the contrary, he seemed rather eager to please his wife. Mrs. Hill fastened Conrad's apron around Mr. Hill's middle, folding it practically in half. Mrs. Hill then spun him around to face Conrad.

"How do we look?" she asked, posing beside her husband with a pert little smile on her face.

"Perfect."

"Betsy," Conrad began, as he leaned back and watched them, "will never make a decent parlormaid. "We can try, but I don't think we'll be successful. I have already made numerous attempts to broach the subject of table settings. But she only stares at me stupidly. She believes there is only one way to set a table. I have told her we are getting new china and that each person henceforth will have approximately twice as many plates before him as he used to. She thinks, however, that the only time more dishes are put on a table is when more people are sitting there."

Mrs. Hill, her arms in dishwater up to her elbows, asked whether it might not make a difference when Betsy saw all the beautiful dishes and glasses. "As you said this morning, perhaps she actually has to see the things before she can believe they exist."

"Possibly," Conrad admitted. "At least we shall try. But I believe we should start grooming Mrs. Wigton for Betsy's work. She can learn. She is an intelligent woman. And then, if Mrs. Wigton proves satisfactory we can let Betsy go."

Mrs. Hill looked thoughtful.

Conrad continued: "Of course, Mrs. Wigton will have to be relieved of some of her other duties. That's only fair. But I'm sure none of them is too onerous or esoteric for someone else to perform. You and I already handle all of the household accounts. Maxfield has nothing to do with them any more and Mrs. Wigton does no more than submit requisitions to you. I

see no reason why she should not be relieved of that responsibility. You know much better than she what is required in the
house by way of repairs, replacements and additions. The mistress always knows, or should know, more than the housekeeper.
Naturally, minor details of the day-to-day household operation
can still be left to her."

Conrad paused.

The two white-aproned figures continued their steady labor.
They were almost through with the dishes, and then there was
the imposing collection of unwashed pots and pans . . .

Conrad got up and ladled himself a bowl of broth.

"Tomorrow," he went on matter-of-factly, "Mrs. Wigton will
be told that she need no longer bother herself with requisition-
ing anything needed outside the housekeeper's room . . ."

"I will have to ask her certain questions," Mrs. Hill said
quietly. "There are some things I'm not completely sure—"

"That's only to be expected. But Monday is the first of the
quarter, and when we do our inventory this time Mrs. Wigton
can get everything ready instead of Betsy, and you can do the
actual tabulating. And while you're about it, tell Mrs. Wigton
about the new dishes and glassware, and the new table settings
we are going to institute."

Mrs. Hill nodded slowly at these suggestions and said she
thought they were very good.

Mr. Hill, who had said nothing up to this point, looked up
from his chores for a moment and smiled at Conrad in a very
friendly way. "Our new dinner settings are coming this Wednesday, aren't they, Conrad?"

Conrad assured him they were.

"I just can't wait!" exclaimed Mrs. Hill. "I'm so tired of all
these old broken and unmatching sets. They're so ugly. I'm surprised anyone has been willing to eat off them."

Conrad sipped his broth.

"When our new settings arrive," he said, smiling ever so

slightly, "we need not fear inviting anyone. We are getting the very best. —Rennie will come down, so will Monte Springhorn, and many more. We will entertain in style."

Mr. and Mrs. Hill exchanged anticipatory glances.

❦

Mrs. Wigton made it clear on Sunday that she did not approve of Mrs. Hill's assuming both immediate and ultimate responsibility for the condition and upkeep of everything necessary to the operation of the household. The table linen, for example: she could not understand why henceforth Mrs. Hill should decide when replacements were required. Surely that was the responsibility of the housekeeper. And the silver polish—that was another thing: why should Mrs. Hill decide when it was getting low? From time immemorial the decision to order new silver polish had been the housekeeper's. And uniforms for Betsy? Mrs. Hill should only decide what style the maid was to wear, and even that decision should be made only after consultation with the housekeeper as to practicability, etc. Mrs. Hill, however, informed her that in the future she would decide when the maid needed something new.

All of Mrs. Wigton's complaints fell on deaf ears. Mrs. Hill merely told her she was being relieved of some of her responsibilities: ". . . not because of incompetence, Mrs. Wigton. I'm sure you'll understand that, but because you will have new duties. It would not be fair to expect you to do both." Mrs. Hill left the new duties unspecified. If Mrs. Wigton wondered what these might be—and she undoubtedly did—Conrad's presence dissuaded her inquiries: he stared at her so blackly every time she raised an objection that she was reduced to making her sentiments known by little else but a persistent and sullen silence.

Her sulking continued through Monday, which witnessed a still further paring of her traditional duties as housekeeper: in-

stead of Betsy getting everything ready for Mrs. Wigton to examine and count—and the results of the inventory then being
passed on to Mrs. Hill—Mrs. Wigton got everything ready and
Mrs. Hill did the actual appraising and tabulating. Throughout
the taking of the inventory Conrad appeared continually and
maintained a watchful eye over all, occasionally giving Mrs.
Hill advice and direction.

At last the dinnerware arrived, in five large crates.

"I think we should have some drinks," Conrad said after the
crates had been set in the dining room. The whole family was
gathered around the crates with the exception of Ester; she had
been told of their arrival but had merely grunted the reply that
she'd see them in due time. Daphne, petite and beautiful now,
was standing close to Harold, her eyes shiny with excitement.

"Daphne, would you care for a drink?" Conrad asked. "And
you, Harold?"

"I never drink in the afternoon, Conrad," Daphne replied
gently. "But if you say it's all right . . ."

"Today is an exception." Conrad turned to Mr. Hill, who was
smiling at him expectantly—almost conspiratorily.

"Shall I serve it now?" Mr. Hill asked.

Conrad nodded without saying anything, and Mr. Hill beamed
and left the room. He returned shortly with a large steaming
punch-bowl—a concoction of fruits and liqueurs, which had
taken him all morning to prepare under Conrad's direction.

"A two-glass limit for Daphne," Conrad said. "For the rest,
the limit is their capacity."

Mr. Hill, smiling and happy, filled everyone's glass.

"And one for yourself," Conrad reminded him.

And so, sipping their drinks, they began the unpacking.

XXIX

The following day when the breakfast things had been all cleared away, Conrad told Betsy that he and Mrs. Hill would teach her how to set the table for lunch in a proper way; the way she had been setting it all along was wrong and no longer acceptable.

"There are many proper ways to set a lunch table," he explained to the sullen-looking maid. "Today you shall learn one of them."

Betsy didn't answer.

Mrs. Hill had stacked the dishes they were going to use on one end of the dining table. The silverware was in a tray on top of the sideboard. "Bring the tray here, Betsy," Mrs. Hill said.

Betsy hesitated for a moment, and then went over and picked up the tray. Conrad watched her closely. As she carried the tray to the table she suddenly stumbled—

Conrad's arm shot out and grabbed the heavy tray with silver, which was just starting to fall from Betsy's hands onto the stack of new dishes . . .

Almost simultaneously Conrad's other hand slapped Betsy hard on the side of her face.

"Don't try that again," he said coldly. "You might lose more than your job, remember that."

For a moment Betsy was too stunned to react, and then, very gingerly, she began rubbing the side of her face, where a large red welt was just beginning to rise.

"Now we shall begin our lesson," Conrad continued. "Mrs. Hill, lay the table so our dear maid can see what settings look like."

Mrs. Hill started to comply, when Conrad stopped her.

"Wait—Betsy, bring Mrs. Hill one of your aprons. —You have a loose dress on, with large buttons," he explained; "and loose clothes with large buttons guarantee breakage: something gets caught in a fold, a button catches on the table-cloth . . ."

Mrs. Hill murmured an apology. "Of course," she admitted. "I should have known better."

Betsy came back with an apron; Mrs. Hill tied it around herself and began to set out the dishes.

Betsy watched; at least, her eyes were directed toward Mrs. Hill's efforts. Every so often Betsy touched her cheek where four finger-length welts had risen.

After Mrs. Hill had laid out six settings, Betsy tried her hand.

"And don't break anything," Conrad warned her.

"Now," Conrad said after Betsy had completed one setting, "let us see what you have wrought. To begin with, why do you have that knife on the left side of the plate? It is not on the left side in any of the other settings. It is on the right side."

Betsy mumbled something about being sorry, picked up the knife and placed it on the other side of the plate.

"That's better. But it is not good enough. The blade of your knife, Betsy, is turned away from the plate. In every other setting it is turned toward the plate. The blade, Betsy, in case my terminology confuses you, is the cutting edge of the knife—you know, the part you saw away with on a piece of meat . . ."

Betsy duly turned the knife around.

"Oh, that's much better. —And now," he continued, "the handle on that cup. In every other setting it is facing to the right. You have the handle sticking out to the left. Do you have some specific reason for your choice?"

Betsy turned the cup around.

"And now the design, Betsy. In every other setting the design on the plate . . ."

And so on, until Betsy's setting closely resembled those of Mrs. Hill's.

"Now, Betsy, you shall lay another setting. Remember, just like the other ones on the table . . ."

The lesson continued till noon.

The family ate off the old dishes at lunch. Conrad said it was necessary to wash all the new dishes and glasses thoroughly. Mrs. Hill said she understood, and asked Conrad whether he trusted Eggy to wash the new things.

"I think it would be better if we did it. Eggy would not understand why things that look clean need to be washed. He might think he was being punished, unjustly. Such feelings could lead to carelessness."

That afternoon Mrs. Hill washed the glasses, and the next afternoon—following another lesson with Betsy—when Mr. Hill did not go to the mill, Mrs. Hill brought him into the kitchen and the two of them, in white aprons, washed all the new dishes while Conrad and Harold prepared the evening's dinner.

Betsy's lessons continued for the next two weeks, but as Conrad had warned Mrs. Hill, they were waging a losing battle with the girl. What she learned one day she forgot the next. Or conceivably, she did learn, but just refused to apply her knowledge.

"And if she can't learn a lunch setting," Conrad said, "she certainly will never manage a dinner setting—not even for the family, much less if we have guests."

Mrs. Hill agreed completely. "I would have to watch her every move," she said. "If I have to do that, I would rather set the table myself. At least that way I won't have to worry constantly that the silly girl might break something."

"Perhaps you're right," Conrad said.

I'm surprised she hasn't broken something already . . . It's only because we watch her like hawks."

"What about Mrs. Wigton—is she proving more tractable?"

Mrs. Hill replied that she was not. "She complains that she has nothing to do now. She said that now that I do everything she doesn't know what's going on in the household. She said she didn't know why we bothered to keep her, that we didn't seem to have any need of a housekeeper. —She is very upset."

Conrad was sitting on his stool and Mrs. Hill was leaning against the kitchen door. "Speaking of not bothering to keep someone," he said; "there's the matter of Rudolph. He was drunk again tonight and of no use whatsoever."

"Yes, he was terrible," Mrs. Hill agreed. "But Benjamin didn't mind doing his work."

"I know."

Just then there was a light tapping on the kitchen door.

Mr. Hill's head appeared around the corner, and he asked timidly whether he might come in.

"I thought maybe Harold was here," he explained apologetically. "I hope I'm not disturbing you. —He's not in his room."

"He's in my room," Conrad said, "studying the books."

Mr. Hill lingered by the door, not knowing what to say.

"Did you want to speak to him?" Conrad asked.

Mr. Hill shook his head and said it was not important. "I was just wondering whether he is going to the mill tomorrow. Did he say anything to you?"

"No, he's going to the mill tomorrow," Conrad answered. "We're having an all-day lesson in basting. Why—is there something important happening?"

"No, no, nothing important. It's just that we were considering some renovations, and I thought . . ."

"Can't someone else handle it?"

"Oh, yes, yes, certainly. It's just that I thought someone from the family . . ."

Conrad glanced at him sharply. "Aren't you going?"

Mr. Hill replied rather sheepishly that he was hoping it wouldn't be necessary. "I actually don't like to go to the mill any more. I don't know why. It just doesn't interest me any longer. I'd rather stay here at the mansion. It's much more interesting here. Something new always seems to be happening . . . things keep changing here. At the mill it's always the same —day after day the same routine. But here . . ."

Mrs. Hill smiled at Conrad. "If Benjamin had his way," she said, "he would never go to the mill again. He much prefers to be here. He likes to do things here—don't you, Benjamin?"

Mr. Hill allowed that she was correct.

"Well, I can understand that," Conrad said. "A household is always more interesting than any kind of business. Probably because it's more personal. It has to do with the very lives of the individuals involved. Business is removed from life. Business is necessary only to support life. It is not an end in itself. Business is a means. The house is the very end, because that is where life is. Or to put it more strongly—it *is* life."

Mr. Hill nodded vigorously. He said that was exactly the way he felt. "Why, I get more pleasure, more personal satisfaction, out of fixing drinks for everyone, or carrying in a heavy tray, than I could ever possibly get from doing anything at the mill. And like cleaning all the new dishes—I enjoyed that! And tonight, when Rudolph couldn't—"

"Good," Conrad said. "But speaking of changes and speaking of Rudolph—that's one change which must be made immediately: Rudolph must leave. He's worse than useless."

Mr. Hill agreed that Rudolph would be released the next day, with a month's wages in lieu of notice.

Conrad said that was perfectly satisfactory.

"There's also the matter of Maxfield," he went on. "He shouldn't be fired. He's just sick. But if he doesn't get well soon, he should be pensioned off."

Neither Mr. Hill nor Mrs. Hill had anything to say against this proposition. Maxfield had been invisible for quite a while, and was practically forgotten. In any case, Mrs. Hill and Conrad had relieved Maxfield of much of his authority. And Mr. Hill enjoyed performing the tasks which had been traditionally the responsibility of the butler . . .

Conrad stood up, and Mr. and Mrs. Hill left.

XXX

Betsy refused to learn her new duties, with the result that Mrs. Hill increased her efforts to groom Mrs. Wigton. Mrs. Wigton, however, proved no less recalcitrant than Betsy; this finally led Conrad to suggest to Mrs. Hill that they talk to her and point out which side her bread was buttered on. "The example of Rudolph might prove instructive," Conrad said.

Rudolph had been fired, as Mr. Hill had promised, and three days later he had frozen to death in the snow within forty yards of the shed, where he had slept for years. Conrad had been drinking at the Shepard's Inn that night, and the dogs had been waiting for him outside the door. There was thus no hue and cry when Rudolph fell in the snow, with a bag of pheasants clutched in his arm for Conrad. Conrad discovered him several hours later, as stiff as a frozen side of beef.

But Mrs. Wigton only broke down and cried when Mrs. Hill talked to her. She said nothing about wishing to comply with her employer's demands. Even the statement that Maxfield was not indispensable hadn't shaken her apparent resolve, and when a few days later Maxfield was indeed pensioned off and removed from the house, she still gave no indication of a willingness to perform the work of a maid.

Maxfield had been deteriorating rapidly. In fact, it seemed as if complete rest and careful feeding were bad for him rather than good, and at last Conrad had suggested that a doctor be called in: ". . . we have done all we can." Mrs. Hill agreed, and Dr. Law arrived very early the next day.

He stayed with Maxfield nearly half the morning. Conrad had prepared a snack for the doctor, and Mr. Hill was just getting ready to take it upstairs when the door was pushed open suddenly, almost knocking the tray from his hands.

Dr. Law strode purposefully to the center of the kitchen. Then he turned around and gave everyone a long, professional look—almost as if he wanted to see if they were sick.

He himself radiated good health, and only his hair suggested middle or advanced years—it was white, snow-white. His neat, forked beard was also snow-white.

Conrad stepped forward. "I was just sending you something to eat."

Dr. Law began balancing lightly on the balls of his feet. "Were you?" he said.

"Yes." Conrad indicated the tray Mr. Hill was still holding. "There are some sweet rolls and butter and coffee."

Dr. Law's eyes did not follow Conrad's to the tray. "I never eat between meals. —Now, about Maxfield," he went on, turning to Mr. and Mrs. Hill. His voice was cold, clinical. "He is too old and debilitated to perform ever again the duties of a butler. I have no doubt of this prognosis. I am positive."

He paused, as if expecting some resistance. But no one seemed surprised by his words.

"Maxfield will be lucky if he can get around without help," he added.

Mr. and Mrs. Hill shook their heads sadly.

"Sometimes it happens," Dr. Law continued. "A man gets old before his time. Maxfield is such a case. He is like a man of ninety. Yet he is several years younger than I."

"A very old ninety at that," Conrad agreed.

"It seems so strange," Mrs. Hill was saying. "I knew he had a bad stomach for some time, but then suddenly he just seemed to age—"

The doctor cut her short. "As I said, Maxfield is senile. He will never work again. Good day!"

Dr. Law left the kitchen as unceremoniously as he had entered, and a few moments later Conrad said he was sure Mr. Hill would rather have someone else break the news to the old butler, so he volunteered to do it himself. "I will spare you that pain," Conrad declared.

Mr. Hill smiled gratefully.

❦

". . . so it's agreed. Four weeks from this Wednesday we shall have Rennie and Monte Springhorn here for dinner. By that time you will be able to manage the two main courses, Harold. Paul will do the pastry; Charles, the soup. I shall do the sauces."

Conrad rose to his feet. Mr. Hill picked up the tray with drinks, and the three of them went into the dining room.

Conrad and Harold sat down at the table—Harold next to Daphne—and Mr. Hill served drinks all around.

Conrad raised his glass. "A toast . . . To the success of our first dinner at the mansion for guests from the City!"

Mr. and Mrs. Hill looked delighted. The glasses were emptied.

"And now a second toast . . . To the success of Harold's first attempt at being in charge of the kitchen."

Mrs. Hill beamed an affectionate smile at her son.

The toast was drunk.

" A third toast," Conrad went on, looking fixedly at Mrs. Hill: "To the success of our new dishes and our new table settings."

Mrs. Hill smiled, blushed, and lowered her eyes.

"Oh, I hope so," she whispered.

"Now," Conrad said after they had all set down their glasses, "let us get on to the actual business of the dinner."

❧

The next afternoon at the Shepard's Inn, Conrad told the other cooks what the menu would be, and said he would teach them whatever was necessary.

Conrad bought Charles and Paul a final round of drinks; then Charles returned to work at the Prominence Inn, and Paul left to do the shopping for Conrad and himself.

"Well, Harold," Conrad said; "what do you think? Are you looking forward to the occasion?"

Harold answered that he certainly was, but that he just hoped everything would go all right.

"Don't worry, it will . . . at least from your end. But Mrs. Wigton—I doubt that she will do." Conrad finished his beer. "But even that's not a problem. Mrs. Hill knows that part of it perfectly. She only needs some practice."

Conrad called to Nell for another round: ". . . and bring that paté over!"

Conrad leaned back in his chair: "Harold, I feel like a young man, and yet, next week I'm having another birthday—I won't

tell you how many I've had before. But every time I have a birthday I feel one year younger.

"It's Friday—a good-luck Friday. I can tell you exactly what
I did the last time it was a good-luck Friday: I spent the entire
day at the Steward's Club in the City with many of my friends.
We talked and sipped wine and liquor until it was dinnertime,
and then I had my favorite birthday dinner. A very simple
dish . . ."

Conrad trailed off.

"Is there anything I can get for your birthday?" Harold
inquired diffidently, handing Conrad a cracker thick with paté.

"Not a thing, Harold. But thank you."

"Oh, but there must be something . . ."

Conrad shook his head. He said the only material possessions
he needed were the tools of his trade—mainly knives and books
—and he already had the best; and the proper attire for dining,
which he had in sufficient quantity and quality. "More than that,"
he went on, "I don't need for my life. With those exceptions,
I have no need of or affinity for material possessions. They
don't interest me. —But let me tell you about my birthday
dinner. As I said, it is an extremely simple dish. I have it only
on my birthday, to proclaim the event and to insure the pleasure
of the dish. It comes from my book on Mountain Peasant Fare,
and it originated in the mountains of . . ."

Harold kept spreading paté on the crackers and handing
them to Conrad.

XXXI

Conrad's doubts about Mrs. Wigton were well founded: Mrs. Hill could make no progress with her; she simply refused to have anything to do with setting a table. "It's not that I consider it beneath me," she declared firmly to Mrs. Hill; "it's just that I'm supposed to be a housekeeper—I'm paid to be a housekeeper —and setting a table is not part of a housekeeper's duties."

And that, for all practical purposes, was that, because, as Mrs. Hill reported to Conrad: ". . . she said I could fire her if I wanted to. But she wouldn't do Betsy's work."

Conrad replied, "We just might do that too."

When Conrad saw the figure for Daphne at the regular Monday weighing session, he told her he would start giving her richer food. "We don't want you to lose any more. If you do, your new clothes won't fit you when they come."

Daphne blushed at this reference to her wedding trousseau.

Mr. and Mrs. Hill recorded slightly lower figures despite the fact that they had extra clothes on: Mrs. Hill had on a full apron and Mr. Hill was wearing a new black jacket with brass buttons.

After the weighing, Mrs. Hill followed Conrad into the kitchen. "Mrs. Hill," Conrad said, "I think we should have a trial run with the Crown Gourmet Setting this Thursday or Friday. —You are sure Mrs. Wigton can't be persuaded?"

Mrs. Hill said she was positive.

"All right, that's settled. Then you're going to have to do it; do you think you can manage it?"

A happy smile lit up Mrs. Hill's face. "I was afraid you were going to say that you would do it yourself, Conrad."

❧

Tuesday night Conrad dined in solitary splendor at the Prominence Inn, and then he went to Shepard's. There were quite a few people there, and in no time at all his table had more chairs pulled up around it than it could comfortably accommodate.

"I hear," said Lem, one of the journeyman carpenters at the mill, "that Mr. Hill never comes to the mill any more. They say Mr. Renfrew does all the work now and makes all the important decisions."

The Hills, of course, being one of the two great families, were always interesting to talk about, and everyone looked to Conrad.

"Mr. Renfrew always did make all the decisions," someone declared before Conrad could answer. "The way I heard it, Mr. Hill just came every day and nosed about, getting in the way . . ."

Conrad confirmed what Lem had been told.

"Yes," someone else said, "it's Dr. Law's orders. He went over to the Hill mansion a couple of weeks ago and said Mr. Hill just had to take it easy. Been pushing himself too hard—he's not the young man he used to be."

Conrad said it wasn't true. "Dr. Law did not say that. Or if he did, he's mistaken. Mr. Hill is in excellent health—haven't any of you seen how he's lost all that fat? He is just bored with mill work, that's all. From now on he will doubtless stay at home more and more, and hand over the actual operation of the mill to Mr. Renfrew—the way the old Cobb family handed over the reins to the Hills and Vales in the first place. History has a way of repeating itself."

Yes, that's true—history does repeat itself, several voices agreed.

"Yes, just look at Ester Hill," said the first man.

"What do you mean?"

"Why, when I saw her and her mother last week," the man answered, "I almost didn't recognize either one of them—you don't see them much any more, you know. Mrs. Hill looked just as trim and neat as a maid—she's really lost weight. And the daughter was just the opposite. Why, Ester Hill is almost as fat as Daphne Vale used to be."

Another man confirmed this, adding, "And I hear tell that Lance Brown is going with a little dairymaid now, and no longer sees the Hill girl."

"I've heard the same thing," said a fourth. "I've even heard that Lance Brown and the girl are secretly married."

"Well, he certainly doesn't come to the mansion any more," Conrad admitted.

"I don't blame him!" said Lem.

All at once everyone was laughing. The table became so boisterous that when more drinks were wanted, Conrad had to call to Nell three times before she heard him.

XXXII

By the time Conrad got back to the Hill mansion it was after three in the morning. He didn't go inside at once. The moon was full and almost bright enough to read by. In the distance the battlements of the Prominence stood out against the silver-black sky. At irregular intervals below the battlements, opaque black shapes gleamed—windows, from which no light ever came, from which no human sounds were emitted, from which no one ever looked . . .

Before retiring for the night he stopped in the kitchen. It was neat as a pin. Everything had been washed and put away. Nothing seemed out of place. Just the way he liked to see a kitchen at the end of the day's cooking, and he guessed that Mr. and Mrs. Hill had helped Harold clean everything up.

Conrad left a note for Harold, telling him to go ahead and fix and serve breakfast. He also wrote out a short menu for him.

Conrad was awake until almost dawn. He had arranged his great long bed so that he could lie on his side and see the Prominence, and until he fell asleep he lay there staring at it. . .

Betsy was let go the following morning while Conrad was still in bed. She had—as Mrs. Hill explained when Conrad appeared—broken one dish too many.

"The wench should have been dismissed months ago," Conrad declared. "There is no place for the likes of her in this establishment."

Conrad took the cup of coffee Mrs. Hill had poured him and walked over to Harold. "How did it go last night?"

Harold replied that it had been a "thrilling experience to be in charge of the kitchen." He added that of course he had only served Daphne what Conrad had already prepared.

After a bit Mr. Hill came into the kitchen. He was wearing his black jacket with the gold buttons. Mrs. Hill told him that Conrad had approved of her dismissal of Betsy.

"Now, about this evening," Conrad began. "The Vales are coming. You, of course, will serve the drinks."

Mr. Hill nodded.

"And you will set the table."

Mrs. Hill smiled and nodded.

"Harold will serve the food. Perhaps tomorrow night, Mrs. Hill, you can serve the food, as well as set the table. It is better not to begin serving when there are guests. Harold has had some experience. —Do you think we should have a trial run of the Crown Gourmet Setting tomorrow night or would you rather serve your first meal with the old dishes, and then on Friday night, having had one experience of serving dinner, try the

Crown Setting? Naturally, you will have served two lunches by tomorrow night . . ."

Mrs. Hill and Harold answered at the same time that they thought it would be better to wait till Friday night to try the Crown Gourmet Table Setting. "I shall have had more experience by then," Mrs. Hill explained, echoing Conrad's words.

"Fine. Then it's settled—Friday night. Harold, you and I have some shopping to do. If we hurry, we can be back in time to fix lunch by one."

Conrad stood up, and as Mrs. Hill turned to leave he asked her whether Mrs. Wigton had been affected in any way by seeing her set the table on Monday. Mrs. Hill shook her head: not in the least. "And I'm not going to ask her again," she declared. "I would much rather do it myself. And if Mrs. Wigton doesn't stop suggesting certain things . . ."

"Yes," Conrad answered, "she had better. —Has she heard about Betsy yet?"

Mrs. Hill said she didn't know, but that she supposed Betsy had run and told her.

"Well, I hope dear Mrs. Wigton draws the correct conclusions," Conrad said.

The problem of who would serve Mrs. Wigton her meals, now that Betsy was gone, was settled by the time Conrad and Harold returned from their shopping expedition to Cobb.

The table for lunch was set and Mrs. Hill was waiting in the dining room, looking very proud of herself. She had on a new white apron, and her heavy head of hair was securely fastened in the back with a broad ribbon.

It was immediately evident that her expression of triumph was due to something other than just the table settings, and after Conrad had glanced at them and nodded his satisfaction, she said, "Guess what?"

Conrad arched a quizzical brow.

"Mrs. Wigton," she declared, relishing each syllable, "has just quit. Not more than fifteen minutes ago . . ."

"This is the way you carry a tray . . . this is the way you fold the napkin . . . this is the way you set a plate . . . this is the way you present the serving platter . . Now, come into the dining room and I'll show you how to set down the tray on the sideboard . . . how to exchange plates . . . how to replace a knife . . ."

Mrs. Hill's instruction was extremely intensive. Before lunchtime, and all that afternoon, and all the following morning and afternoon, Conrad taught her as much of the art and as many of the tricks of serving as she could conceivably assimilate in that short period of time. She was a willing and apt student, and when it came time to serve dinner Thursday night Conrad assured her—because she was a little nervous—that she would acquit herself creditably. And it was true: except for a few minor confusions involving the entremets, dinner came off without a hitch. Mrs. Hill was extremely pleased.

❧

Friday morning Conrad slept late again; he had gone to Cobb after dinner to have a few glasses of beer at the Shepard's Inn and to talk and listen to the local gossip.

Harold and Mr. and Mrs. Hill were in the kitchen when Conrad came down, and as soon as he appeared the three of them chorused:

"Happy Birthday, Conrad!"

He smiled and thanked them, saying quietly, "I'm glad you reminded me. I had forgotten."

Mr. Hill pulled Conrad's high stool over to the side, and Mrs.

Hill served him his coffee and his favorite semisweet rolls, and then, as Conrad sipped his coffee and began to dip the bread in it, Harold said, "Conrad, today there will be nothing for you to do. It is your birthday, and we will take care of everything in the house. This evening—I would feel highly honored if you would let me cook dinner for you . . ."

Harold started to say something else, but became covered in confusion and broke off.

Conrad dipped another piece of bread in his coffee and answered mater-of-factly that he would be pleased to have Harold cook for him. Harold and Mrs. Hill sighed with relief.

Conrad started for Cobb about an hour later. Just before he left he sought out Mrs. Hill and told her that he had heard last night from a reliable source that Lance Brown was secretly married to a dairymaid.

Mrs. Hill was overjoyed.

"Should I tell Ester?" she asked.

Conrad replied that she should tell her immediately.

❧

Conrad returned from Cobb carrying a small suitcase. Dinner was at nine. When he appeared downstairs, dressed for the occasion, he caused a sensation: could this be Conrad the cook?

Mr. Hill indicated the chair at the head of the table.

The new dinnerware was on the table. The setting was the Crown Gourmet Table Setting Number Two.

Mr. Hill poured Conrad a glass of dry sherry.

Conrad sipped it, ran his tongue over his lips, and nodded his approval.

Mr. Hill, standing ram-rod straight beside the chair, seemed a little relieved, though it was difficult to be sure because his expression was so fixed. The gold buttons on his black jacket looked as if they had just been polished.

"Mrs. Hill," said Mr. Hill quietly, "asked me to tell you that Daphne will not be dining tonight. She is indisposed."

Conrad nodded.

"And the cook wishes me to tell you that he has prepared for you your birthday dinner, the one you told him about. He made it on Tuesday when you were in town, and he thought it came out all right. The second time, he thought, it would probably be even better."

Conrad nodded but said nothing, and Mr. Hill stepped back out of sight.

Conrad sipped his sherry. When his glass was only one-quarter full he cocked a forefinger at it very unobstrusively. Mr. Hill silently stepped forward and refilled it.

The large grandfather clock at the end of the room began to toll the hour of nine. Before it had finished Ester walked slowly into the room. Mr. Hill stepped forward and drew out the chair on Conrad's right.

Ester was huge. She was wearing a green satin gown with large red roses all over it. Conrad recognized the gown as one Daphne used to wear.

"Sherry?"

After a moment Ester seemed to nod assent, and Conrad raised a finger toward her glass. Mr. Hill stepped forward.

When they had finished their sherry, Conrad said quietly to Mr. Hill, "Any time now."

Mr. Hill returned shortly, followed by Mrs. Hill. She was wearing a black and white uniform. Her cap was fringed with stiff lace.

With an expression of fixed concentration she approached the table.

On the small silver tray there was an assortment of . . .

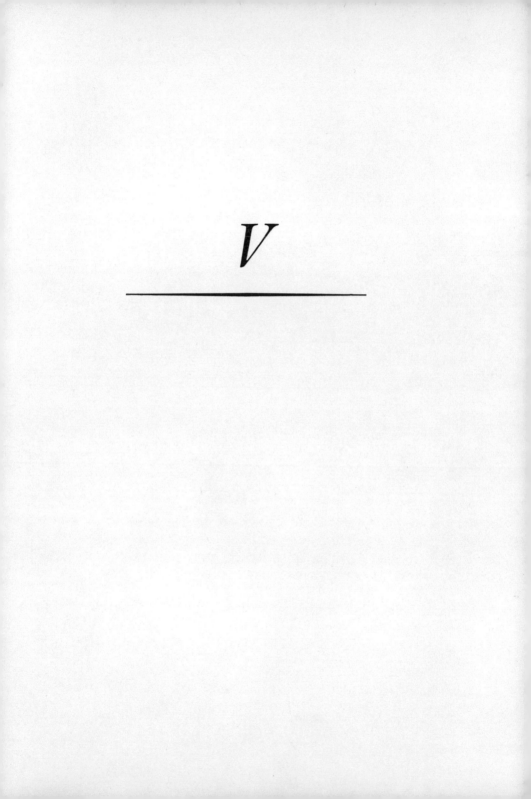

V

XXXIII

Conrad's birthday dinner was the first rehearsal for the coming major performance for Mr. Bayard and Monte Springhorn. The following week another rehearsal was staged when the Vales were over for dinner. Mrs. Hill explained to them what they were doing and why Conrad would be sitting at the head of the table. Mr. and Mrs. Vale—plump and jolly now—thought the whole thing was a wonderful scheme and entered happily into the spirit of the evening. Conrad was his usual charming dinner self, and combined with the transformation wrought by his evening clothes, in no time at all he had both the Vales figuratively eating out of his hand. Everyone had a wonderful time. There was only one discordant note: Daphne Vale was still indisposed and could not come down for dinner. But as if to make up for this, fat Ester made her appearance and was again seated on Conrad's right.

❧

At last the big day arrived. Conrad slept late that morning, and when he came down for breakfast Charles and Paul were already in the kitchen going about their duties.

Eggy was busily at work in the corner by the sink. His stool had been taken away to make more room.

"We're trying to keep out of each other's way," Harold smiled, coming up to Conrad quickly and handing him a cup of coffee and a small plate of buttered sweet bread.

"Just don't panic. There's enough room in here for eight cooks. But each must tend strictly to his own business."

"Yes, Conrad . . ." Harold agreed over his shoulder, continuing what he had been doing.

Just then Mrs. Hill rushed in. At the sight of Conrad she gave a quick sigh of relief. "Ah, I'm so glad you're here! I was so afraid I'd forget something." She reached into her apron pocket. "Here—last night I was too nervous and excited thinking about today to sleep. So I got up and made a list; I wrote down everything I've done and everything I've got to do . . . I think. Would you look at it?"

Conrad smiled and glanced at the top of the first page. It was headed: "Guest room for Mr. Monte Springhorn." Halfway down the page was the second heading: "Guest room for Mr. Rennie Bayard." Under each were subheadings: "Linen," "Wardrobe," etc.

Before Conrad could turn to the second page Mr. Hill came in, and the sight of him seemed to remind Mrs. Hill of something. She exclaimed abruptly that she would be right back and rushed out of the kitchen.

Mr. Hill was looking tense with suppressed excitement and at the same time somewhat worried, though he was trying to hide this even more than his excitement. For a few seconds he just stood there watching Conrad go over Mrs. Hill's long list.

"Yes?" Conrad murmured, not looking up.

Mr. Hill began to finger one of his gold buttons. "Mrs. Hill wanted me to make a list too. But I think I work better if I just keep going over things in my head—that's the way I used to do it at the mill. But there are so many things to do . . ."

"Each person has his own method."

"But I think I know what I have to do. But—"

"Yes? But what?"

Mr. Hill continued to finger one of his buttons. Then at last he answered. "It's not that I don't believe . . . I mean, it's not that I don't think your friends . . . but, Conrad"—and with much effort he forced himself to raise his eyes to Conrad's—"but, Conrad, do you *really* think Mr. Springhorn—and Mr. Bayard—will come to the mansion today . . . I mean, all the way out here from the City, just to have dinner at *our house?* Mr. Springhorn is such a *great* man. *Such* a great man . . ."

Mr. Hill's voice had dropped to a murmur. He sounded almost disconsolate, and his eyes pleaded with Conrad to dispel his doubts.

"We're always anxious," answered Conrad quietly, "when we're anticipating something greatly. That's partly what it means to anticipate. And that's part of the fun: the pitch of our anxiety is the measure of our anticipation, not of the likelihood of its fulfillment. —Mr. Springhorn and Mr. Bayard will be here between two and three this afternoon. Rest assured."

Mr. Hill considered Conrad's words for a moment, and then began to nod. "Well, I must admit I'm really looking forward to having Mr. Monte Springhorn here, and Mr. Bayard . . ."

Conrad patted Mr. Hill on the shoulder and said with an easy-going laugh, "You had better be careful now. And Mrs. Hill. Two o'clock is a long way off. If you don't calm down a little, the two of you will work yourselves into such a state of nerves that you'll be desperately hoping Monte and Rennie won't show up. That happens, I know: at one of my first big dinner parties I caught myself making a solemn vow to eat all of the food I had prepared if only my guests would not appear. I didn't want to see them—that's how convinced I'd become that all of my dishes would be a failure. But of course, all the guests did come, and they ate everything set before them. The dinner could not have been a greater success—and the occasion today will be just as successful." Conrad laughed again. "And tell Mrs. Hill what I just said: not to get too excited. Everything will work out perfectly. We have planned things down to the last—"

Mrs. Hill burst through the kitchen door. "Conrad! Conrad!" Her eyes were wide with distress. "I just examined the table-cloth again and look . . . look—right in the center—I didn't see it before . . ."

She held up the delicately ornate table-cloth, all starched, and beautifully white. Only—in the center there was a large, solid black spot.

"What shall we do? What shall we do?" Mrs. Hill was on the verge of tears. "I just put it away last night—I don't know how it got there. But it must be my fault. I just don't see . . ."

Conrad took one sharp glance at the spot and then leaned back against the cupboard.

"Mrs. Hill, I was just telling Mr. Hill not to let himself get too worked up about today. The same goes for you. Otherwise you'll be in a state of nervous incapacity by this evening—do you want Eggy to serve our guests? That would be a tragedy. But the tragedy you're pointing to is only a spot of black candle wax, no doubt dropped by you when you put away the cloth last night. It can be scraped off in a minute."

Mrs. Hill looked again at the spot, and then heaved a huge sigh of relief.

"You see," Conrad continued, finishing his coffee; "we mustn't let ourselves get too excited. Everything has been planned very carefully for today and all will go well. Our two distinguished guests are in for a treat."

Mrs. Hill, still not fully recovered from the shock of finding the spot on the table-cloth, was able to do no more than nod weakly at Conrad's reassurance.

Conrad stood up. "And now we must all get on with our work. Just remember, take everything in stride and don't get too excited. That's the rule."

Mrs. Hill nodded again.

"And if small things go wrong, always remember: they're small. They can be tended to."

⁂

Everything was in order by two o'clock.

"Now we are ready," Mrs. Hill smiled.

"Yes . . . see? I told you everything would be all right." Conrad turned to Mr. Hill, who was rearranging once again the numerous bottles on a large serving tray. He did not look happy. "Our guests will come," Conrad assured him.

Mr. Hill said nothing.

The three of them were in the kitchen, keeping out of the way while Harold, Charles and Paul went about their tasks.

"Perhaps," Conrad suggested, "our cooks would like something to drink? Mr. Hill . . ."

Mr. Hill fixed three drinks, and then one for Conrad and one for Mrs. Hill.

By two-thirty Mr. Hill was looking more despondent than ever.

"I know you think they won't come," Conrad said. "But they have another half-hour before they're even late."

"Of course they'll come," Mrs. Hill exclaimed quickly. "Benjamin, you shouldn't be so pessimistic. He *is* being pessimistic, isn't he, Conrad?"

Mr. Hill muttered something inaudible.

"Oh, I don't know," Conrad answered offhandedly; "it is not unknown for guests to disappoint."

Mr. Hill, who had continued to move the bottles around on the tray, looked up quickly at this flat acknowledgment of possibility. He opened his mouth to speak, but at that moment there was a loud knocking at the front door. Slowly Mr. Hill closed his mouth, but he continued to stare at Conrad and didn't move. The sound seemed to have rooted him to the floor.

The knocking, louder and quite imperious, sounded again.

"Our guests," Conrad murmured.

"Oh, Benjamin!"

With a final tug at the back of his jacket, Mr. Hill left the kitchen.

"Oh, I do hope they find their rooms satisfactory," Mrs. Hill said quietly, more to herself than to Conrad, who had turned to Harold. Harold had been slowly stirring a sauce, but at the sound of the knocking he had stopped, and he was looking almost pleadingly at Conrad. "Yes, Harold, by the time this evening is over you will have gratified two of the most exacting palates of the City."

"But, Conrad, suppose . . ."

The sound of voices came from the dining room, and then the kitchen door opened and Mr. Hill reappeared. Carefully, very carefully, he drew the door closed behind him. For a moment he just stood there. Then he leaned back against the door.

His expression was blank. Indeed, it was more than blank. He looked stunned.

"Well, aren't you going to announce the guests?" Conrad asked.

Mrs. Hill, who had been observing her husband closely, glanced nervously at Conrad. Harold, too, began to look a little concerned. He came over and stood beside Conrad.

"Benjamin?"

Mr. Hill at last collected himself, and taking a deep breath, intoned: "Mr. Monte Springhorn. Mr. Rennie Bayard. And five of Mr. Springhorn's friends."

Dead silence followed this announcement. And then Paul, who had been putting something in the oven, stood up and gave a low whistle.

"Five?" Charles exclaimed. "Did you say five more people?"

Everyone was staring at Mr. Hill.

"And *five* friends," he repeated.

"Damn!" exploded Conrad loudly. "Damn Monte Springhorn and his confounded tricks! I'm going to—" He started for the kitchen door. Mr. Hill moved quickly to one side, but then Conrad stopped. In a lower voice he said, more to himself than to anyone else, "I should have expected something; I know him so well: 'Food' "—and he imitated a high-pitched voice—" 'tastes better when prepared under stress.' One of his ridiculous theories. Only this time he's gone too far—Harold, bank the stoves. There will be no—"

Mrs. Hill leaned back weakly against the cupboard. "Oh, what shall we do? What shall we do?"

Conrad was staring blackly at the kitchen door. He had not completed his sentence: a roar of laughter had suddenly come from the dining room.

"There are five extra guests?" Harold seemed incapable of assimilating the information. He just stood there, looking from Conrad to Mrs. Hill, who had started crying, then to Mr. Hill. Mr. Hill was still staring straight ahead, unseeing. Charles and

Paul looked stunned. They had stopped what they were doing and came over to Conrad. Only Eggy took Mr. Hill's announcement in stride; mumbling that more people meant more dishes, he bent closer over the pile in the sink. But the others didn't hear him, and shaking their heads, they began muttering unhappily.

"There just isn't enough food," said Harold.

"No, not near enough."

"And I have only prepared two guest rooms. Oh, Conrad—"

"We won't have enough time either. If we had more time . . ."

"If it were just one extra person it would be different. But five—"

"No one can expect us to take care of seven when we were only preparing for two," Charles said. "I know at the Prominence Inn, when twice as many people come as—"

Mr. Hill nodded at this statement. "Yes, they will have to go to the Prominence Inn. There is no other way."

"Oh, the Prominence Inn!" exclaimed Mrs. Hill through her tears. "When the Vales find out . . ."

But Conrad was looking sharply at Mr. Hill. "No one is going to the Prominence Inn—except Charles to pick up some things from their emergency stock. We are going to take care of our guests just as if they were all expected. There will be no panic. Mrs. Hill, start preparing additional guest rooms. Paul, get ready to go to the Vales' for some fish . . . and possibly some extra bed linen—ask Mrs. Hill. Explain to Harold what you have cooking, and what he must do while you're gone. Charles, you do the same. I will be back shortly to write a list of the items I want you to bring from Cobb."

Conrad paused and gave a long, hard look to all of the faces around him. They all still looked pretty blank. Mrs. Hill, though, had stopped crying.

"As I said"—and Conrad's lips parted in a slight smile, with just a trace of warmth—"there will be no panic. Dinner will be perfect. —And now I must welcome our guests. Mr. Hill, you will serve the first two rounds of drinks. Then you can help Mrs. Hill till I come back to the kitchen."

Monte Springhorn was very short, very wide and very thick, so that he quite resembled a cube. His head, in contrast, was round, and it sat on the block of his torso without evidence of attachment by any length of neck. He was completely bald.

Bright, mischievous eyes sparkled at Conrad as he introduced his five friends.

"We've all met before," Conrad smiled. "I'm pleased you were able to get the little party together, Monte. Did you have any trouble?"

Monte Springhorn chuckled to himself, his heavy jowls trembling like jelly. "No, no trouble at all," he said in his shrill voice. "I simply mentioned you were having a little dinner and sought the pleasure of some City company. And having eaten at your table before—well, naturally they were delighted. Why, were you afraid Rennie and I might have to make the trip by ourselves?"

"I'm honored," Conrad said to the others. —"Yes, I'll admit the possibility had occurred to me."

Springhorn chuckled again. "Yes, I suppose one never knows what to expect. The world is full of surprises."

Conrad opened his mouth to reply but changed his mind, and smiling slightly he took Monte Springhorn by the arm, suggesting that they all sit by the fireplace.

Mr. Hill served drinks. He was the perfect stony-faced butler: he seemed to look at no one and yet at everyone at the same time. And when he wasn't actually serving he was out of sight. Indeed, if it hadn't been for all the shiny gold buttons against the background of black cloth, he would have melted so com-

pletely into the room's furnishings that had one of the guests
looked for him he would have looked in vain.

"Gentlemen"—Conrad raised his glass to each in turn—"I'm
so glad you were able to come. —Now, what has been going on
in the City? Rennie, have you had anything decent to eat since
you were in Cobb last?"

The five unexpected guests, all portly gentlemen, turned
pleasantly to Rennie Bayard and exclaimed almost in chorus,
"Tell Conrad about your friend who is being charged with
attempted poisoning. He's just been telling us," they explained
to Conrad.

Rennie Bayard laughed. "All right, all right—" He leaned
back comfortably in his chair. Mr. Hill was standing behind
Conrad, and surreptitiously Conrad handed him a note—a
change in the evening's schedule. Only Monte Springhorn saw
this, and his high-pitched chuckle accompanied Rennie's open-
ing remarks about a recent dinner he had attended. "It seems,"
Rennie began, "that unbeknown to the host, the chef had once
been employed by the guest of honor, a gentleman of rather short
temper and unlimited fears, who had discharged him for something less than just cause. Or so the chef felt, and upon learning
that this gentleman was to be . . ."

When the laughter had quieted down, Monte Springhorn followed with another tale of catastrophe striking an unsuspecting
host. Soon everyone was talking, their voices rising in order to
command attention, Conrad's no less than the others', as all tried
to tell a story which in some wise exceeded the one just previously related. Of course, it wasn't long before all of the stories
began to sound apocryphal . . .

Conrad served the third round of drinks, and Monte Springhorn said, "Oh, has the butler left us?"

"That's your drink, Monte. —He has standing instructions to
leave after the second round. I prefer informality."

"An excellent notion," commented one of the other guests.

"Yes; and I suppose he has better things to do—there are always last minute matters to attend to, small changes in plans, et cetera."

"Yes, of course, Monte. —But you were saying . . . ?"

Monte Springhorn waited till Conrad had served everyone and had sat down again. "Yes, I was saying . . . Conrad, do you remember that strange chef I once had? I forget where I found him now—I had him for such a short time. The one who created the most marvelous and unusual sauce?"

Conrad smiled over the rim of his glass. "So you said . . ."

"What sauce was that?" Rennie Bayard asked. "Did I ever taste it?"

"No, Rennie, you never did. —Yes, Conrad, so I said. Well, gentlemen, let me tell you what happened. I gave a little dinner, just for a few friends, to show off this incredible sauce . . ."

Mr. Hill materialized behind Conrad and they exchanged a few whispered words, then Mr. Hill vanished.

". . . and this guest that Conrad brought—I don't know who he was—he was the first one to receive the large sauce-boat, the very first one. However, I will say this: the sauce-boat was round, perfectly round. And the ladle in it wasn't too large, not too large."

"The meats, Monte—don't forget to tell them about the meats."

"Oh, yes, the meats. There were three kinds of meat, each one bone-dry. It had taken the chef hours and hours to get them so dry, which, of course, was part of the secret of the astonishing success of his sauce. Well, these meats were so dry . . ." He dwelled over the dryness of the meat to such an extent that Rennie Bayard soon had an empty glass. Conrad refilled it just as Monte was finishing his story.

". . . Conrad's friend set the sauce-boat in front of himself, pushing his plate of dry meat to one side, and proceeded to ladle the sauce into his mouth like soup! Everyone was too stunned to do anything but watch him, slack-jawed."

Monte Springhorn joined in the laughter that followed the telling of his story. When at last he could catch his breath, he concluded: "The chef came out a short time later to receive our blessings, and when he saw all the plates of untouched dry meat and then realized what had occurred, he removed his chef's cap and stalked straight out the front door. I never saw him again."

"Oh, what a shame! And you never learned the secret of the sauce?"

"Never."

"I never saw my friend again either," Conrad smiled. "I've always suspected the sauce killed him. —Gentlemen, if you'll forgive me—it seems my presence is desired in the kitchen. I shall be back shortly."

Monte Springhorn's high-pitched chuckle followed Conrad out of the room.

At six o'clock the guests retired to their rooms to rest briefly and to dress for dinner. Five extra guest rooms were ready. Monte Springhorn inspected each one, and when he came down to dinner he took Conrad aside and quietly, and a little grudgingly, complimented him on the measures taken to make his friends comfortable. "I suspect it took some doing," he added slyly.

"It did. But with a willing staff one can work wonders."

"True. But it has been my experience that staffs are rarely willing."

"It all depends. You shall see when it's time to eat."

The dinner was a complete success. The food was excellent and more than plentiful. And the serving was immaculately

executed—Mrs. Hill was faultless in her performance, as was
Mr. Hill in serving the several wines which accompanied the
courses.

Daphne, unfortunately, was indisposed and could not come
down, but Ester was there, and she enjoyed the dinner and the
conversation and laughter so much that she stayed up several
hours past her usual bedtime.

Monte Springhorn was extremely impressed—rather against
his will, it seemed—because he waited till the very end of the
dinner before vouchsafing to Conrad any words of satisfaction
or praise. But then he capitulated, and with unconcealed admira-
tion admitted to Conrad that all had gone perfectly ". . . and
under what must have been very trying circumstances." He
apologized with a chuckle for being responsible for these diffi-
culties. "But my friends will never know they were unexpected.
You've done a remarkable job."

Conrad smiled. "I'm glad to hear that, Monte. It gives me
great pleasure. But why don't you thank the staff? It was really
their doing."

Springhorn replied that he would indeed like to thank them.
Conrad passed on his wish to Mr. Hill, and a few minutes later
Mrs. Hill was standing beside the dining-room table. She was
beaming with happiness. Harold stood on her right. Charles,
Paul and Eggy were next. Mr. Hill, utterly expressionless, stood
a few feet to the left of Mrs. Hill.

"You did a wonderful job," Monte Springhorn declared, "truly
wonderful. I thank you for all of us. Being a host myself quite
often, I realize"—he paused and gave a little chuckle—"some
of the problems you faced . . . things don't always go precisely
as you planned. In such circumstances staffs frequently go to
pieces. Some of my own have done that—deserted the host, as
it were." He paused and chuckled again. Turning to Conrad,
he continued, "I don't know how you do it, Conrad. In the City,
where one should be able to assemble the finest, it is rare to find a

staff thoroughly first-rate. Here in Cobb I would have thought it completely out of the question. But, Conrad, somehow you managed. It's beyond me."

Springhorn turned back to the group standing beside the table.

"How does Conrad do it?" he smiled. "What is his secret? I should like to take it back to the City with me."

Harold, looking pleased and proud, glanced at Mrs. Hill for a moment and then stepped forward.

"Sir," he said quietly, "we like our work. Naturally we like to do it well."

Monte Springhorn smiled benignly at the young man. "Yes, perhaps the people in the City don't like to work," he admitted.

And then Mrs. Hill stepped forward and said, in a voice that was little more than a whisper, "We love Conrad."

Springhorn's round blue eyes grew wide at this statement. Slowly he then looked at each person standing before him. They all seemed to be nodding slightly.

The dinner party did not break up until four in the morning. After seeing his guests to their rooms, Conrad went back to the kitchen and congratulated the staff himself. He said they had done a wonderful job. It was quite late—he acknowledged, smiling—and he knew they must be very tired. He would talk to them tomorrow after the guests had left the mansion. But again he wished to say: they had done a truly superb job.

XXXIV

The next day Conrad, Mr. and Mrs. Hill, and Harold discussed the great dinner in minute detail. There was much to learn from it and Conrad wanted to drive home every lesson. And they had many questions they wanted to ask him.

Also, Monte Springhorn's words of praise were repeated and repeated . . .

When at last Conrad was alone with Mrs. Hill he said that he had spoken to Monte Springhorn about Daphne's frequent indispositions and continued weight loss.

"Monte said he knew the best specialists in the City. They will be out here within a fortnight."

"That was very thoughtful of you, Conrad," Mrs. Hill said.

"I'm more worried than I'd care to admit. Also"—and her eyes hardened slightly—"it gives me something to tell Eva Vale."

Conrad looked at her inquisitively.

"She's been after me to call in Dr. Law; every time I see her she mentions it. 'I do wish you'd call in Dr. Law, just to examine the girl. I'd feel so much better'—though she knows we're taking the best care of Daphne. Only—"

Mrs. Hill laid down the cloth she had been polishing the glasses with and turned to Conrad; she seemed eager to discuss the subject, yet uncertain how to continue.

Conrad crossed his arms and leaned back against the cupboard.

"Do go on, Mrs. Hill," he said, his black eyes beginning to glow with an unusual intensity. "I find what you're saying most interesting: 'only' *what*?"

"Only—well, I certainly don't see what Dr. Law could do. He didn't do anything to help her before—under his care she just got fatter and fatter, until she was as fat as a pig. And I don't see why—" Again Mrs. Hill broke off.

For a moment Conrad said nothing. He seemed to be thinking. Then he said, very slowly, "You are so right, Mrs. Hill. You are so right: as fat as a cow."

"Yes, like a cow."

"Perhaps, Mrs. Hill," Conrad continued, still measuring his words very slowly, "perhaps Dr. Law wants to fatten her up again, the way she was before—have you thought of that?"

"Oh, Conrad!" Mrs. Hill looked at Conrad despairingly.

"All our work undone . . ."

For several seconds the two of them communed with each other in silence, seemingly sharing a vision of an elephantine Daphne. Once or twice Mrs. Hill shook her head and muttered something under her breath. Then she picked up her polishing cloth and began twisting it.

At last Conrad spoke: "We cannot afford to trust Dr. Law."

"No."

"Besides, specialists from the City are coming out."

"Yes."

"And maybe they can help Daphne."

Mrs. Hill had stopped twisting her polishing cloth. She was looking quite happy again, and Conrad smiled at her. Then, pointing a finger for emphasis, he said, "You must tell Mrs. Vale."

"Yes, I certainly will. I will tell her today."

"You must tell her"—Conrad pointed his forefinger straight at Mrs. Hill's eyes—"that we do not trust Dr. Law, and that we refuse to call him in. He is not acceptable. He was not able to help Daphne before. He was not able to make the Vales healthy. For years he treated Maxfield for his stomach, and look what happened to him. Such is Dr. Law's past—hardly something to inspire confidence, is it?"

"No, it is not."

Conrad lowered his finger and smiled warmly at Mrs. Hill. "Shall we drink to that? Shall we drink to the rejection of Dr. Law? It seems appropriate, don't you agree? And I know just . . ." He turned around and removed a tall, narrow-necked bottle from the top shelf in the cupboard. "This will do fine."

Mrs. Hill got the glasses Conrad told her to—long, slender ones—and held them out to him. He filled each one to the very brim. Then he took the one she was holding in her left hand, and bending down a little, put his arm around her shoulder.

They touched glasses.

❈

Thursday evening of the following week Daphne's recorded weight was one hundred and eight pounds. The Vales were over that night, and when Daphne said she felt too tired to stay downstairs for dinner, Mrs. Vale became very upset.

"Indeed, it was all I could do," Mrs. Hill reported later, "to keep Eva Vale here; she wanted to send for Dr. Law immediately. I had to remind her that specialists from the City were coming. She couldn't seem to remember. She kept repeating Dr. Law's name, and I had to tell her over and over that Dr. Law was not—"

"You did very well," Conrad assured her. "The specialists will be here tomorrow."

The next afternoon four somberly attired, serious-looking gentlemen arrived.

"We have been sent by Mr. Springhorn," the oldest one announced. "Where is the patient?"

They spent several hours alone with Daphne, and when at last they repaired to the dining room it was time for pre-dinner drinks. Mr. Hill served them, explaining that Conrad would be in shortly.

Two of the specialists sat and two stood. They talked in low tones and shrugged frequently. One of them held Daphne's weight chart in his hand. Every so often the other three would consult it, and then sigh and shrug in unison.

After a while Conrad arrived and the specialists spoke quietly to him for about an hour.

When they were through, Conrad thanked them and said that business was over for the day.

"It is time to enjoy ourselves now," he smiled. "Gentlemen, tell me about yourselves . . . Do you all know Monte? . . . And how did you get interested in the fine art of dining—or, as some prefer to put it, the refined science of gluttony?"

Soon the four specialists were all laughing and talking at once.

Throughout dinner they talked and laughed, and Conrad regaled them with gourmet stories till after midnight. So lighthearted and gay was the company that again Ester stayed up way past her bedtime.

※

Saturday morning at ten o'clock sharp Mr. and Mrs. Vale arrived. Mr. Hill let them in and took them to the dining room, where Mrs. Hill, Conrad and Harold awaited them.

There was a seriousness about the Hill group which the Vales—plump and jolly though they were—immediately sensed and their smiles faded away. They took the chairs Mr. Hill indicated, and said nothing.

Conrad presided. He waited till all were settled.

"I will repeat," he told the newcomers, "what I have already told Mr. and Mrs. Hill and Harold. Four specialists examined Daphne yesterday. Four of the top specialists from the City. They substantially agreed on their findings: something is wrong with Daphne but just what they haven't the slightest notion. Nor have they any idea what to do. Diet was the one thing they had in mind, but when I told them what she was eating they answered that that was precisely what they would have prescribed. They had no suggestions."

Slowly, ever so slowly, two tears rolled down Mrs. Vale's plump cheeks. She whimpered something about wishing she could give her poor girl some of her own weight.

"I'm sure we all wish the best for her," Conrad said in a very matter-of-fact voice.

He continued, "The doctors had some advice, non-medical. I told them Daphne was engaged to be married in June. They said there was no medical objection to her marriage. But they advised—all four of them—that the marriage not be delayed till June. They did not give their reasons. There was no need to."

Mrs. Vale began crying uninhibitedly.

Conrad ignored her.

"I assume," he went on, "that we're all agreed the marriage should take place as soon as possible."

Everyone nodded.

"Good. Now, her clothes already need altering. We can get Louise busy on them immediately. How soon," he asked, looking at Mrs. Hill, "do you think we can have the wedding, all things considered?"

Mrs. Hill wrinkled her brow thoughtfully, and then began counting on her fingers. "To be on the safe side, Conrad," she answered at last, "I think we should say about four weeks. That way . . ."

The Vales stayed for lunch. The only subject of conversation was the wedding; the problems attendant upon advancing the date, the usual myriad of details, etc.—and Mrs. Vale soon became her jolly self again, dismissing from her thoughts the specialists' visit and what they had said. Nor did she take notice of Daphne's absence from the table. Of course there was no unused place setting drawing attention. But the prospective wedding alone seemed to occupy her. And it was only when she was leaving, after she had gone upstairs to say good-by to her daughter, that Mrs. Vale seemed to recall why they were all talking about the wedding . . .

❧

The wedding was also in Mrs. Hill's thoughts to the virtual exclusion of all else, and hours after the Vales had left she was still talking about it, planning it and replanning it, seeing it one way and then seeing it another. It did not seem to matter whether anyone was listening, though occasionally she would ask Conrad if he agreed or what he thought about something.

"What should we have to drink at the reception?"

Conrad was leaning against the cupboard, glass in hand; dinner was almost ready and Mr. Hill had just fixed drinks, reminding Mrs. Hill that this was an aspect of the wedding affair she'd overlooked.

"I suppose," Mrs. Hill said thoughtfully, answering herself, "that we should have something of everything, shouldn't we, Conrad? After all, we want to celebrate an occasion which—" She was interrupted by a knock at the front door.

"I wonder who that can be? At this time—"

Mr. Hill left immediately to find out.

"Conrad, who do you suppose . . ." Mrs. Hill trailed off as another voice was heard—someone had come in—and a few moments later Mr. Hill reappeared.

He closed the door firmly behind him. His eyes met neither Conrad's nor Mrs. Hill's. Then he announced, in an utterly impersonal voice: "Dr. Law. He wishes to see Conrad."

Mrs. Hill's mouth fell open.

"Dr. Law!" she exclaimed. "What is he doing here? No one asked him . . ."

"Dr. Law," repeated Mr. Hill impassively.

Conrad was still leaning against the cupboard sipping his drink, but he was looking past Mr. Hill at the door leading to the dining room.

Mrs. Hill turned to him. "Conrad, what do you think . . ."

Conrad continued to stare at the door. Then he finished his drink in a swallow, and straightening up to his full height, said, "Mrs. Hill, Dr. Law said he wished to see me, not Daphne. But perhaps he meant he wished to see me first. Therefore, I think you should go upstairs—patients often like to be at their best for the doctor. You understand? Just tell Daphne that Dr. Law is here."

Dr. Law was standing in the center of the room, arms crossed, balancing lightly on the balls of his feet. He was staring into the fireplace. Idly, as if from habit, his right thumb and forefinger were twirling the tip of the left fork of his beard.

At the sound of footsteps Dr. Law spun around, and in the directness of his gaze upon Conrad there was something of a challenge.

"Seat?" Conrad suggested, nodding toward a chair by the fire.

"I always stand, thank you."

Conrad sat down in the chair across from the one he had indicated. "Something on your mind?"

Dr. Law smiled professionally. "Yes, there are several things. Are you surprised?"

Conrad sighed and stretched his legs out toward the fire.

"No," Dr. Law said after a moment, "I don't think you are surprised. You have probably been expecting—"

"Get to the point, friend."

Dr. Law's smile vanished. He looked very hard at Conrad. "The point is this, sir: I see through you. You are not fooling me."

Conrad glanced up at him. "Congratulations."

"And I don't like what I see."

"Then don't look."

Dr. Law peered at Conrad very intently. For a few seconds he even discontinued his bouncing movement, as if he had to be perfectly still to get Conrad in proper focus. At last he said, almost admiringly, "You're very sure of yourself, aren't you?" And when Conrad didn't answer: "You're certain no one can touch you. You've taken care of everything. You've thought of all the possibilities. You have left nothing to chance. Nothing can change the course of events . . ."

"Except you, Doctor," Conrad said in a bored voice; "is that what you're trying to say?"

"You *are* very sure of yourself."

"Bluff, Doctor. All bluff."

"Possibly *too* sure. —No, not all bluff. If that's what it was you'd be correct in your statement: I would do something about it; I would have done something before now. But it's not that simple. Not that simple at all—"

Dr. Law paused. Conrad had turned away from him and was looking into the crackling flames, which made shadows dance across his face, distorting and concealing his expression. Dr. Law moved a step closer. Cocking his head to one side, he tried to see through the shadows to Conrad's face. Slowly Conrad turned from the fire to look at Dr. Law. For a few seconds the two men examined each other.

"I am not your friend, sir," Dr. Law stated abruptly. "I want you to know that. Indeed . . ."

Conrad turned back toward the fire.

"It's not something personal, not at all: no more than, as a doctor, I am a *personal* enemy of disease. But I'm not its friend and I do fight it. And I hope the word doesn't offend you. I mean nothing more by it than . . ." Dr. Law paused for a moment, evidently intent that his words convey precisely his meaning. "A disease," he explained after a few thoughtful tugs at his beard, "is simply something to be treated and, if possible, eliminated. That is, after it has been diagnosed. If it cannot be eliminated it should be contained. If not contained, then inhibited. And so forth. At all events, it is not to be encouraged.

"Treatment follows diagnosis," Dr. Law continued. "Diagnosis is simply recognizing the existence of something and calling it by its proper name.

"And now I will be perfectly frank. It isn't always obvious what treatment to use. And sometimes the doctor calls in a consultant. Occasionally there are no consultants to call. And other times there is no doubt as to the prescribed treatment, only it cannot be counted on to work. It depends on the individual case. And in very rare instances it seems there is no treatment at all. Only diagnosis . . ."

Dr. Law trailed off meaningfully, and Conrad, who had slid down so that his shoulders were almost on the seat of the chair, turned over on his side and looked at him. " 'Seems,' doctor? I gather you're not certain."

"No, sir, I am not. I am still hopeful. Having made the diagnosis, one can scarcely rest content . . ."

"And you have come to *me* for help? There are no consultants to call on this case—"

"I know that, sir."

"I am glad. There is no one to help you, doctor. No one at all. You are alone. Just you and your diagnosis."

Dr. Law began bouncing up and down more vigorously. Then he nodded slowly, evidently agreeing with what Conrad had just said. "Then why, sir," he asked, "do you think I have come here? Granting, that is, the diagnosis—I mean yours—of my impotency."

"Possibly," Conrad murmured, half turning back to the fire, "you were just passing by."

"No, I can assure you I came here quite on purpose."

"Well, let me guess again: to exhibit your cleverness. You have come up with the perfect diagnosis . . . you alone—and of course such a feat should not pass unappreciated. So you come to me. Also, you have a nagging suspicion there's nothing to be done. At least nothing you can do. And still, as you said, you are not without hope: it occurs to you that perhaps *I*, perhaps Conrad, can do something. That's possible. Anything is possible. Do I have to make a third guess, doctor?"

Conrad wasn't looking at the doctor—indeed, his eyes were almost closed—and when Dr. Law didn't reply immediately, he added: "You're very proud of your powers of observation, aren't you? Very proud—probably even a point of honor with you. 'Others may be blinded. Others may be taken in. But not I. No, sir, not I'—not the good old doctor."

Dr. Law smiled his professional smile. "It is pleasant to know," he allowed, "even when one is not quite sure what to do. But as you observed, I am hopeful. And I will further admit that the pleasure of knowing is increased by recognition: I appreciate your admitting my comprehension of all—"

"You don't know, Doctor," Conrad said bluntly; "you don't know at all. You don't even listen to me when I talk—I said you came to convince me of your brilliance. You failed. You and your diagnosis . . . you couldn't diagnose a case of hanging!" Conrad turned and faced the doctor. "You can leave now."

Dr. Law stopped bouncing, and the smile disappeared from his face. "What did you say? What did—"

"My dinner is waiting," Conrad returned casually. "I don't know about you, Doctor, but cold food tries my temper."

For an instant the doctor seemed to doubt his hearing. And then: "Sir, you are . . ."

But Dr. Law evidently didn't trust himself to speak: indeed, the twin points of his beard were quivering like the prongs of a tuning fork in vibration.

"What am I, Doctor? Tell me—what's the professional classification? I'd like to know." But when Dr. Law didn't answer immediately Conrad got to his feet. "I'm tired of waiting. Good night."

"Just a moment!" Dr. Law quickly interposed himself between Conrad and the door. "I have not done with you, sir. Not by any means. I will not tell you what you are. Name-calling is both unseemly and unprofitable. But this is what I wish to say. My diagnosis is not wrong. And what is more—this may surprise you—I have a treatment. I am not *absolutely* sure of its efficacy. But I have the highest faith. Sir"—and Dr. Law took a half-step toward Conrad, which required him to bend his head almost straight back to look up into Conrad's eyes— "sir, I demand to see Daphne Vale. At once."

Conrad cocked his head slightly, as if trying to get someone so much smaller than himself in focus. Then he bent down and laughed in Dr. Law's face.

Dr. Law held his ground. "This is scarcely a laughing matter. You know that as well as I do. But you have overreached yourself—a not uncommon mistake among the confident. And you shall pay the price. —Sir, I repeat: Daphne Vale is my patient. I demand to see her at once."

"She is not your patient."

"She is, and as her doctor I demand to see her."

"Impossible."

"I insist. I shall not leave this house till I do."

"And suppose you are put out?"

"I shall come back. And I shall bring Mr. and Mrs. Vale with me."

Conrad stepped right up next to Dr. Law. "And just what good would that do?" And he bumped the doctor a little.

"Sir, they are her parents."

"So what? Who cares?" Conrad bumped the doctor harder, and Dr. Law had to take a quick step backward to keep from falling over. No sooner did he recover his balance than Conrad's hand shot out to grab him—

"Conrad!" Conrad spun around quickly; it was Mrs. Hill. She was standing in the deep shadow at the foot of the stairs. Beside her, all in white, was Daphne Vale.

"What are you doing down here?" Conrad demanded angrily. "You know better than—"

"Daphne!" came the startled cry from Dr. Law. "Is it really you? I can't believe it! My dear . . ." and he started across the room toward her, but Conrad grabbed him by the arm and jerked him back. "Stay where you are. Daphne requires complete rest. Mrs. Hill, you know what the specialists said."

"Conrad, we decided to come downstairs," Mrs. Hill explained somewhat nervously. "I told Daphne that Dr. Law was here and she insisted." Mrs. Hill turned to the young girl. "Now, Daphne, dear, don't you think . . ."

Ignoring the restraining hand Mrs. Hill held out toward her, Daphne Vale slowly crossed the room.

"How are you, my dear?" exclaimed Dr. Law, incredulous at what he saw. He grasped one of her hands between his own and patted it very affectionately. "How are you?"

Daphne smiled, most beautifully, and replied that she was extremely pleased to see Dr. Law; she added, in a slightly teasing voice, "Mrs. Hill said you had gotten some grave reports about me, that I was ill and dying and that you had come to see for yourself. Well? How do I look? Do I look unwell? Or unhappy?"

Daphne Vale looked truly radiant, physically fine and in the highest of spirits, and Dr. Law was unmistakably nonplused. Slowly he shook his head. "I have never seen you looking so well. Or so beautiful. I don't understand it—you have changed so. And I received such reports from your mother and father . . ."

Daphne laughed gayly. "I have never felt better in my life, Doctor. —I am going to be married soon."

Dr. Law nodded. "I know that, my dear."

"I shall be Mrs. Harold Hill."

"Yes, my dear, I know. And no one could be more happy for you than I . . . But, Daphne, tell me something"—and Dr. Law gently grasped the girl's elbow and led her into a darkened corner of the dining room, out of earshot of Conrad and Mrs. Hill.

The grandfather clock struck eight-thirty.

"Yes, Doctor," Daphne was saying. "I'd rather be Mrs. Harold Hill than anything in the world. Anything, Doctor, anything. Can you understand that?"

They had returned to the center of the room. Dr. Law was twirling the left point of his beard. He looked very grave . . . or very serious . . . or very dubious—or weary.

"I don't know," he murmured. "I don't know."

Daphne moved away from his side.

"And I am going to have what I wanted. Things have changed. I am getting my wish."

Dr. Law said nothing. Daphne glided over to Conrad, who was leaning against the dining-room table. She turned and held out her hand to Dr. Law.

"I am extremely happy."

Dr. Law took her hand. Then he turned to Conrad.

"This is all your doing, sir . . ."

Conrad looked at him coldly. "Are you asking me or making a statement?"

"Good night, Doctor," Daphne said quietly.

"I don't know, sir," Dr. Law said. "I really don't know."

He turned back to Daphne. "My dear, I wish you the very best . . ."

Mrs. Hill accompanied Dr. Law to the front door. As soon as it closed on him Conrad turned to Daphne. She looked at him for a moment, trying to smile. Then her eyes rolled back in her head and she sank to the floor unconscious.

"Get Mr. Hill to carry her upstairs," Conrad said. "You come into the kitchen with me. Some changes will have to be made in serving, which often happens when a dinner is delayed . . ."

XXXV

From the time it had been decided to advance the date of the wedding, everyone in the Hill household was extremely busy. Louise was brought over the very next day, and she began getting Daphne's trousseau ready. The regular members of the household set about planning and getting ready for the wedding itself and for the move to the Prominence.

Conrad went to Cobb to consult the lawyer who was the present executor of the last Cobb's will, because the first thing to find out was where the wedding should be held: at the Prominence or in either of the mansions. Conrad said the Prominence would be preferable, if legally possible, because of the symbolic significance: the Prominence had been the home of the Hill and Vale forebears and would henceforth be the home of the Hill and Vale descendants, and so it should be the situs of the unification of the past with the future. On the other hand, both the Hill and Vale mansions were literally negative symbols: each proclaimed the schism. As for getting married in a public place—where could a suitable one be found in Cobb? And as for going to the City and holding it there—that too was out of the question, if for no other reason than the bride's state of health. She was much too delicate to undertake such a journey. Indeed, her condition also excluded the traditional honeymoon trip. Conrad had talked this over with Harold, and they had decided it would be best to take up residence at the Prominence immediately after the wedding rather than tax Daphne's strength with all the exertions of a honeymoon.

The lawyer decided there were no legal impediments to the performance of the marriage at the Prominence. This pleased Conrad immensely. The lawyer also told him something about the last Cobb's will: any of the surviving Hills and Vales who chose to reside at the Prominence after the joining of the two families had to provide in *his* will that all of his property should pass, on his death, to the bride and bridegroom, and then to their heirs and descendants, except for life interests and limited legacies to their children and certain collateral heirs. The purpose of this provision was obvious: to join the estates together, just as the families had been joined, so that the last Cobb could finally rest in peace, secure in the knowledge that he had succeeded in passing down intact the vast Cobb holdings.

Conrad reported this to Mr. Hill and asked him whether he was aware of the provision. Mr. Hill answered that he hadn't looked at the will for many years but that he thought he remembered something of the kind. Anyway, his own will would only require a few minor revisions for compliance.

"Does Mr. Vale know about it?"

"I don't know, Conrad."

"Then perhaps we should get him over here for a little talk."

When Mr. Vale came, Conrad told him about the provision, and then added, "I assume we are all going to move to the Prominence. There seems no point in maintaining these separate mansions. They represent a family feud which is much better forgotten."

Mr. Vale, fat and friendly, looked a little puzzled at these words.

"But, Conrad," he remonstrated mildly, "I thought it had already been decided that we would all move to the Prominence—Eva has spoken to Mrs. Hill about it many times. I thought it was just taken for granted that that was what we all wanted."

"Good," Conrad answered. "That's all I wanted to hear. —You understand the provision of the will?"

"Yes, certainly," said Mr. Vale. "But it doesn't make any difference to me. I've already made my will, leaving everything to Daphne, or in case she marries, to Daphne and her husband, and their heirs. All that remains to be done is to insert Harold's name in the document."

Conrad replied he was glad to hear that there was no impediment to the Vales' taking up residence at the Prominence immediately after the wedding.

"None whatever," agreed Mr. Vale. "In fact, that's what we've been doing all these weeks—getting ready to move from our mansion to the Prominence. That's a lot of work, Conrad . . ."

❧

No one was working harder than Harold Hill.

After Harold and Daphne had become engaged and the move to the Prominence had been assured, Conrad and he had many discussions about the great kitchen there. Conrad still refused to visit it, saying there would be plenty of time, but he told Harold that a kitchen such as he described was a godsend, both to cooks and diners, and that not to employ it to capacity would constitute a rejection of a gift of the gods; surely calamities would follow in the wake.

"Great cooks," Conrad said, "require great kitchens. And vice versa. They also require great diners, and ditto vice versa. Harold, you will be a great cook. The Prominence kitchen shall make you one. And you, in turn, will make it great—no, I mean it," he said as the young man tried to demur; "I absolutely promise it. When we get to the Prominence you'll see what I mean. Meanwhile, we must make all preparations and learn as much as we can. Here, at the Hill mansion, you can only learn how to cook and to be responsible for the dishes. It is not feasible to have you supervise other cooks—besides, first things first. There will be time enough at the Prominence for you to learn to be in charge of other cooks . . ."

It was in this context—the pending move to the Prominence— that Harold had begun to do more and more in the kitchen. There was no time for him to go to the mill any more and he didn't try to make the time. When he wasn't in the kitchen or on a shopping trip, he was in Conrad's room poring over the books. And after he had been shopping with Conrad the two of them would go to the Shepard's Inn, and while Conrad drank a few beers and gossiped with whoever was there, Harold would sit in the corner and read one of the cook books he had brought with him.

And then, when the wedding date was suddenly advanced, Harold's efforts to perfect his skills so that he could move into the Prominence kitchen and try to do it a little justice, became positively frantic: if he could have absorbed all that was in Conrad's books and at the same time spent twenty-four hours a day in the kitchen—if this had been humanly possible, without doubt Harold would have done it.

XXXVI

"The wedding will be a very small affair, just the families and the best man."

Conrad leaned back and called to Nell for another round of drinks.

He had just told everyone that the wedding between Daphne Vale and Harold Hill was to take place a week from the coming Thursday and not two months hence in June, as all had thought. The news caused quite a sensation. He explained that the change in announced plans had not been made public because not till yesterday had the actual date become certain; all had hinged on some special clothes for the bride. These had arrived yesterday from the City.

"Why the rush?" someone asked. "I thought June was the month for weddings . . ."

"The health of the bride-to-be," replied Conrad quietly. "It is delicate, and daily grows increasingly so."

Several of the men expressed amazement at this. Looks passed back and forth among them.

"We heard nothing about that," said one of the men. "Everyone thought, now that Miss Vale isn't fat any more she is in good shape."

Conrad smiled and said that the secret had been well kept. "You see," he explained; "now that Rudolph, Maxfield, Betsy and Mrs. Wigton are gone, there are no sources of information at the Hill mansion. Eggy, of course, is still there, but he sees no evil and speaks no evil. Whatever is known in Cobb about the goings-on at the Hill mansion must be learned from one of the Hills themselves, from Daphne or from me. There is no other way of finding out."

Yes, that made sense.

"Conrad," said one of the men, "you said the wedding would be a family affair except for the best man."

The speaker paused, and waited till Conrad nodded that he was quoting him correctly.

"All right then, Conrad—who is going to be the best man? That's what I want to know."

"Yes—who is going to be the best man?" asked several voices at once.

Conrad picked up his stein and blew the froth from the top. Then he drank it all off and set it down with a bang.

"I am, gentlemen—I'm going to be the best man! Nell! Bring us another round!"

XXXVII

Conrad talked to the workmen who were responsible for the maintenance of the Prominence grounds and the upkeep of the castle itself, and told them he wanted everything in perfect order for the wedding. Mr. Hill accompanied him when he talked to the men, and then both Mr. and Mrs. Hill went with him when he visited the Prominence to decide in which room the wedding should be held.

It was the first time Conrad had approached the Prominence since that day when he had initially set eyes on it from the road and had sought out the narrow stairway that led up the cliff face to the plateau. Several workmen and two supervisors

went along with them. One of the supervisors carried the key
for the drawbridge mechanism.

Conrad spent about two hours going through all the rooms
and halls of the great Gothic structure. However, he spent at
least half of that time in the great kitchen . . .

As they descended the narrow stone staircase, Conrad,
squeezing down sideways, smiled and said, "I think the Vales
are a bit too plump to negotiate this passage."

Mrs. Hill laughed and said she thought so too.

"We shall have to bring ladders for them," suggested Mr.
Hill very practically and seriously.

And though no one said it, it was obvious that Ester would
also require a ladder.

Indeed, at the rate Conrad had been gaining . . .

❧

Conrad's correspondence with people in the City, always very
heavy, had been increasing steadily over the recent weeks. And
then suddenly it doubled, and then tripled, and practically every
night, after giving Harold instructions for a dish to work on,
Conrad would retire to his room to read the stack of letters
which had arrived that afternoon, and to answer another stack
which had come the day before. Often he was occupied with this
work until three or four in the morning.

Mr. Hill, upon whom had been devolved the responsibility of
bringing in the mail and putting out the letters which were to be
picked up by the postman, knew of course of the sudden increase
in Conrad's correspondence. But he said nothing about it to
Conrad. Indeed, he almost never initiated a conversation with
Conrad; he waited till he was addressed. But he did tell Mrs.
Hill, who casually mentioned to Conrad that she didn't see where
he found time to answer so many letters. For her part, she said,
she was so tired at the end of the day—what with learning all

the new table settings he was teaching her and then actually laying them, and serving the meals and then doing all the washing-up, with help from Mr. Hill and Eggy, naturally; plus all the work involved in getting ready for the wedding and the concomitant move to the Prominence—that when she left the kitchen at night and went to her room, she literally fell into her bed and slept a dreamless sleep till the next morning when it was time to get things ready for breakfast.

"If I had to answer letters, Conrad," she concluded, "I'm afraid I'd lose all my correspondents. I'm simply too worn out at night . . . Although, I suppose, if the letters were really important . . ."

Her curiosity about the letters was patent. Conrad answered that they *were* important, otherwise he certainly wouldn't be sacrificing his sleep for them. But he did not elaborate on this statement, and it was not until shortly before the wedding day that Mrs. Hill found out what all the correspondence had been about.

The family, including Ester, were gathered in the dining room—Conrad had told them he had something to impart.

He sat at the head of the table. In front of him were two stacks of letters, with their respective envelopes attached.

"In a few days," he began, tapping the stack on his left, "we shall be moving to the Prominence. It is an enormous place, and even if we did not plan to entertain, it would take more than just the four of us, plus Eggy, to run it in the proper manner. But since we do plan to entertain"—and his eyes darted quickly to the other packet of letters—"of necessity we need an augmentation of the present staff; I gather that's understood."

Mrs. Hill furrowed her brow, and then her worry expressed itself: "You don't mean you're going to take Betsy back?"

Conrad shook his head impatiently. "Certainly not. There are no servants in Cobb I'd dream of taking into the Prominence, with the exception of two cooks: Charles and Paul are going to assist Harold in the great kitchen. The rest of the staff is coming from the City—that's what these letters concern, Mrs. Hill."

Mrs. Hill smiled with half-satisfied curiosity as Conrad untied the string, picked up the top letter and started reading the qualifications, experience, etc., of a Mr. Breen, who was to be Mr. Hill's assistant. Nominally Mr. Hill would be in charge of all the staff. But Breen would be actually responsible, and it would be his duty to train Mr. Hill to take over in fact as well as in title. Breen would be given six months to accomplish this.

Conrad then read out the qualifications of a Mrs. Thorn, whose duty it would be to train Mrs. Hill. Mrs. Thorn, too, would be given about six months.

Conrad picked up the next letter . . .

When he had finished reading the stack of correspondence it was obvious he had assembled a most professional staff, and Mr. and Mrs. Hill were looking extremely pleased. They had listened very attentively, frequently nodding and smiling, but never once interrupting.

Ester evidently hadn't listened at all; she just sat there, directly opposite Conrad, staring straight ahead, either at him or through him. If there was any expression on her face it was one of slight dissatisfaction.

Harold hadn't listened either, not even when the letters concerned the additional cooks Conrad was bringing into the kitchen: spread out on the table in front of him were half a dozen cook books, and Harold was immersed in them to the total exclusion of everything else.

"Now," Conrad said, "we have finished with these"—he retied the packet and pushed it to one side—"and we come to these . . ." And he drew the other stack toward him. "These you shall see in a moment—but first, let us contemplate the wedding day. Let us try to get it into perspective, and not just our own, because it presents two faces: one to us and the other to the people of Cobb—and very prominent guests from the City." This was the first mention of any people coming from the City and Mrs. Hill opened her mouth to exclaim, but Conrad continued without pause: "We want both of these faces unexceptionable. For Cobb, the Hill-Vale wedding shall be the most important social event of the generation. It must live in their memory. We must put on a notable performance—a perfect performance."

Mrs. Hill, who was still smiling at the pleasant surprise of City guests, nodded in agreement. Then almost at once her expression changed. "It's a shame Daphne is in such delicate health. A proper wedding in the grand ballroom with hundreds in attendance . . ."

"Of course. Everyone likes a great wedding."

"Oh, I know they do. And it's been so long since there was one in these parts. So very long. —Well, we'll just have to make it up to them with the reception. That's all we can do."

Conrad's eyebrows arched disdainfully. "Ah, yes, the reception. Too bad even that can't be perfect: a reception without a receiving line leaves something to be desired. And as for Harold standing there alone . . ." Conrad paused, and then when Mrs. Hill began slowly shaking her head, he continued, "The townspeople expect a receiving line—to pay their respects to the new mistress. They would cherish that experience. It would be something to tell their children . . ." He paused again, and Mrs. Hill watched him as he began tapping the table with the packet of letters. "Oh, I know," she said slowly, "that everyone will want to see her."

"That's part of the delight of the reception, to contemplate the bride . . ."

"I know . . . oh, Conrad, it's such a shame. No receiving line. I feel as if we're letting the people down—almost as if we're taking something from them."

"They'll doubtless share that feeling. And that's not all, Mrs. Hill: what about the other high point of a reception? What about that?"

Conrad paused, but Mrs. Hill just looked back at him without answering.

"What about the cake, Mrs. Hill? What about the ceremonial cutting of the wedding cake? Not to have even that . . ."

Mrs. Hill began to look very sad.

"I'm afraid," Conrad said, "that it would look peculiar if Harold grasped the knife and cut it all by himself. Indeed, most peculiar. Even portentous, possibly—that is, to simple-minded countryfolk. Besides, Harold, are you looking forward to the reception? It will last all day, at least—Harold!" Conrad had to call Harold's name several times before drawing the young man's attention from the cook books. Conrad repeated his question.

"But you know I'm going to be in the kitchen," Harold objected quietly. "I have things to cook. I can't go milling about with the guests. It's out of the question. In fact"—and Harold glanced anxiously at the clock—"I have something on the stove now—if you don't mind . . ."

"Not at all, Harold, not at all . . ."

Harold quickly gathered up all the cook books and left the room.

"So you see," Conrad shrugged; "from the point of view of the guests, the wedding day will be less than complete: no reception line, no cutting of the cake. Indeed: 'Where are the luminaries?' They won't even see them! And then of course, Mrs. Hill, from our point of view we shall have failed: we shall have given less than we promised. And the Hill-Vale wedding day will not be something to remember joyfully. On the contrary, it might even be something to forget . . ."

Mrs. Hill was staring down at the table. Slowly, without looking up, she said, "What you say is true, Conrad. Only too true. I've tried not to think of these things. I have pushed them out of my mind. Somehow, I suppose, I thought they would all be taken care of. I know that was foolish, but . . . I just wanted to think that the wedding day would be perfect, and I couldn't bear thinking that—"

Mrs. Hill broke off, as if too dispirited to continue, and even Mr. Hill, who usually masked his emotions perfectly, began looking a little dejected. Only Ester seemed unmoved by the conversation, continuing to stare straight ahead, and even when Conrad began looking directly at her, very intently, it was still not possible to tell where her gaze rested or whether she was aware of his observation.

"Yes, indeed," Conrad said at last, picking up the packet of letters again and beginning to tap the table with it. "Yes, indeed, some wedding day. Don't you think, Ester? Won't it be great? Aren't you looking forward to it with eager expectation? You must be. It will be a great day in your young life, moving into the Prominence . . ."

"And the guests from the City," Mrs. Hill said sadly. She was staring at the packet of letters in Conrad's hands. "What will they make of this? No bride or groom—coming all the way from the City and not even seeing . . ."

"They could drop in at the sick chamber or the kitchen," Conrad suggested.

". . . they won't even be at the reception. And a reception without a receiving line—and without a wedding-cake ceremony. What will those people think of us?"

Conrad smiled coldly. "What indeed, Mrs. Hill? Because you are correct: these letters are acceptances of invitations from people in the City. From the best people in the City—the very best—and we cannot let them down. Or perhaps I should say"—Conrad's gaze rested for a moment on each of the Hills—"we *will* not let them down. We will *not:* they shall have their luminaries. They shall have their bride and bridegroom."

Conrad rose to his feet and pushed his chair to the table.

Then he stood behind it, hands resting on its back. "There shall be a magnificent wedding . . ."

Slowly, intently, Conrad scanned the Hills. Mr. and Mrs. Hill were looking at him fixedly, the latter frowning slightly. Even Ester seemed to be looking at him.

Conrad spoke again: ". . . followed by a great reception. There will be a receiving line. There will be a fine wedding cake. It will be cut by the bride and bridegroom."

He paused for a moment, and then concluded:

"The wedding day shall be perfect."

The three Hills continued to stare at him silently. In appearance, Conrad was not quite the same as when he had arrived in Cobb. Most striking, he was no longer gaunt and starved-looking. Not that he was fat, but it was his size that would catch the eye rather than any want of proportion: before, he had only seemed very tall and thin; now he looked huge, which made his presence more powerfully felt. His face, too, was fuller and, consequently, less eagle-like in aspect. Yet, this impression remained quite evident: his nose, which really gave his face its cast, was still sharp and hooked, even though it was broader and not so pointed. Still, it was unmistakably a beak. Indeed, if anything, it was a slightly larger and more forceful beak, as befitted the greater bulk of his figure. His eyes, of course, were as black as ever. That some of the lines around the corners had been smoothed didn't seem to change their expression: they were still disconcertingly piercing.

As for Conrad's attire—he still wore black clothes. Only, now these were of excellent fabric and set off by a dazzling white expanse of shirt front, which, as much as the weight he had gained, proclaimed the favorable change in his estate.

It was on this white patch that Ester had had her eyes leveled the entire time Conrad was seated. And when he had stood up, it had drawn her gaze up with it. Only a moment later her eyes had moved to Conrad's face . . .

For several seconds Conrad just stood there, leaning slightly on the back of the chair, looking at each of the Hills in turn. Then his eyes came to rest on Mrs. Hill.

Slowly then, ever so slowly, a smile commenced lighting up his dark countenance . . .

Conrad picked up the packet of letters and tossed them over to Mrs. Hill. Then he walked around the table and stood beside Ester.

"Read the first letter, Mrs. Hill," Conrad said. "Read it out loud."

But Mrs. Hill just stared at the packet of letters, afraid to discover the contents.

"Mrs. Hill—we are waiting."

Gingerly, then—indeed, Mrs. Hill was shaking a little—she picked up the letters. They were tied together by a thin red ribbon, and as she tried to undo it all her fingers became thumbs.

"It's only a bow, Mrs. Hill; I tied it myself. Just pull one of the loose ends. That's right—"

Mrs. Hill removed the ribbon. Shaking still more, she unfolded the first letter. But when she tried to read it she couldn't make her eyes focus.

"Read it, Mrs. Hill. Read it so we can all hear."

Mrs. Hill blinked her eyes several times. Then she held the letter out before her and started to read in a nervous and unsure voice:

". . . pleased to attend the wedding of Miss Ester Hill to Mr. Conrad Venn.

". . . will attend the reception.

". . . accept offer of accommodation at the Prominence."

For a moment Mrs. Hill didn't seem to realize what she had read. Then her breath came in a sudden gasp and the letter fluttered from her fingers to the table.

"The other letters are of the same purport," Conrad said. "There are several more packets upstairs—these are only from

the most prominent people. You'll notice the date, Mrs. Hill—
it's the same as for Harold and Daphne."

Slowly Ester turned her head around.

"Yes, Ester," Conrad said, grasping her firmly by the shoulder,
"we are getting married. You and I." Hesitatingly Ester smiled
at him. "Conrad . . ." she whispered. And she started to raise
her hand to place it on his, but then she changed her mind and
let it fall back on the table.

Mr. and Mrs. Hill were coming slowly toward Conrad. Mr.
Hill had his arm around his wife, as if to comfort or support
her, or give her courage. They stopped just in front of Conrad.

For several seconds they just looked at him.

And then—

Mrs. Hill began smiling at Conrad, through her tears.

XXXVIII

"Our marriage," Conrad said later that evening, "shall be a surprise for the townspeople. Instead of being deprived of what they have every right to expect, they shall be treated to a proud wedding and a most sumptuous and unstinting reception. Moreover, that it comes as a surprise will both increase the pleasure and fortify the recollection . . ."

Mr. and Mrs. Hill agreed completely.

And indeed, the townspeople did not learn there were to be two weddings till the very morning of the great day, when they began arriving at the Prominence and overheard the talk of the people from the City: the City people spoke only of the Venn-

Hill wedding. And though at first little notice was taken of this—the townspeople thought either they hadn't heard correctly or that the City visitors were slightly mistaken—finally some clarification became necessary. For the townspeople were speaking loudly to each other of the Hill-Vale wedding so that if a mistake existed it could be corrected; yet the City visitors persisted in referring to it as the Venn-Hill wedding, and they too were raising their voices, also doubtless to rectify.

"It's *Vale*, not Venn. *Vale*," affirmed one of the townspeople at last. "You're saying it wrong."

The City gentleman thus addressed started to walk away, but several Cobb people gathered quickly around him, and all began repeating the name Vale.

"Daphne *Vale* and Harold Hill," added the man who had first spoken. "It's the Hill-Vale wedding."

"That's right," declared an old woman standing beside him. "Daphne *Vale* and Harold Hill are getting married today."

"Not Venn," said another voice. "*Vale*."

The City man, rather mild-looking and middle-aged, was still half inclined to walk away without replying—what was there to say to such people? They would believe what they wanted to. But on the other hand, they meant well . . .

Smiling tolerantly, he withdrew an envelope from the pocket of his jacket. He turned it over several times, as if to make sure it was the right one; then he opened it and extracted an embossed card. He read the few lines of print on it with scrupulous attention.

"I am here," he said at last, "to attend the Venn-Hill wedding. And so are my friends—so is everyone from the City. We are here at the invitation of the groom. We know no one else. If there are any other weddings hereabouts, so be it. It does not matter. We are interested only in Conrad's." And with that he handed his wedding invitation to the person nearest him. "You may let the others see it," he added, as he heard someone from the back of the group still complaining that the City gentleman had the name wrong.

It was not the City man's words, but rather the written invitation—the coupling of Conrad's name with Ester's—that made the townspeople understand. And they stared and stared at the names on the card, in benumbed silence, until its owner had to ask for it back: the townspeople had forgotten about him . . .

"Could Mr. Conrad Venn be Conrad the cook?" they asked.

But to ask the question was to answer it.

The Hill-Vale wedding was a very quiet affair. Indeed, it resembled a funeral. The bride, who now weighed little more than one hundred pounds, looked very tired and weak. She had a difficult time standing without assistance, and when her father gave her away, he literally handed her to Harold—she had to be passed gently from one arm to the other.

Only the two families and Conrad and Louise were present. Though Conrad had employed a resident nurse from the City to look after Daphne, it seemed advisable to keep Louise on until Daphne had made the adjustment from maiden to wife. And since Louise was to stay for a while at the Prominence, she might just as well be invited to the wedding.

The ceremony itself lasted only a few minutes. Then Daphne retired to the bridal chamber in the north wing, and Harold changed clothes and went to the great kitchen.

The Venn-Hill wedding was something else entirely. It resembled a coronation, as several of the guests from the City commented. Of course the people from Cobb had never seen any-thing like it.

It was held in a great chamber occupying the entire top of the highest tower, which by virtue of the majesty of its view over the surrounding countryside seemed made to order for the crowning of kings and queens. On all sides light streamed in through tall pointed windows. One end of the ballroom was particularly bathed in the bright sunshine, and there a large high dais had been placed. Its steps were covered with purple velvet.

On the dais were two enormous thrones, their backs more than eight feet high and their broad flat arms at least two feet wide. They were of solid rose-yellow gold. The bride and bridegroom were seated on these gold thrones and looking out, as it were, over their massed subjects.

"My, it certainly is different," Louise whispered to Dr. Law, who was standing beside her.

"I should say it's different! There's scarcely anything re-sembling a traditional wedding. There's a man dressed in black and a woman dressed in white. That's all that I recognize. —And all that martial music! I don't believe the people of Cobb ever heard such music before."

Louise nodded—the music was responsible for her presence. She had been tending to Daphne when the sounds of trumpets and drums penetrated the bridal chamber, and Daphne had in-sisted that Louise attend the wedding. "Then you can come back and tell me all about it," she explained, as Louise looked re-luctant to leave her. "And you needn't worry about me. I'll be all right. I'll sleep."

Hurrying upstairs to the tower ballroom, Louise met Dr. Law.

"I thought it would be in the chapel," he explained. "Then I heard the music . . ."

"The chapel wouldn't be big enough," Louise answered.

The tower ballroom itself was extremely crowded, everyone standing except the bride and bridegroom. The guests from the City were all up front, close to the dais; the townspeople were in the rear, and Dr. Law and Louise squeezed themselves in among them. "You just missed the wedding march," a young woman said to Louise. "It was wonderful."

"I heard it, but I was in such a hurry that I got lost—this place is so big. You must tell me about it later. My mistress will want to hear."

"You should see the bride's train!" exclaimed another woman. "It was so long! I've never seen a train so long . . ."

Louise nodded knowingly. "I helped to make it."

"You did?"

"Yes, I stayed up all last night finishing it . . . We had to order more material from the City and it didn't arrive till yesterday morning."

Louise felt a hand on her arm and turned; it was Mrs. Wigton. The ex-housekeeper was looking quite happy, and she and Louise gave each other an affectionate little hug. "It's very exciting, isn't it?" Mrs. Wigton said. "I've never seen anything like it. And look at Miss Ester! This is the first time I've ever seen her smile so happily in all the years that I've known her! Even as a child she didn't smile like that . . ."

Louise whispered confidentially, "If you knew how many yards and yards and *yards* of cloth it took to make that girl's gown! Well, you simply wouldn't believe it—and I don't mean just for the train either."

A stout middle-aged woman made her way over to them. "Have you ever seen Conrad so beaming?" asked Nell. "I never have."

"You better call him 'Mr. Venn,' " Mrs. Wigton reminded her.

"He's very handsome when he smiles," said Louise.

"Yes, he is," the other two agreed. "Extremely handsome . . ."

"Most people are when they smile," interjected Dr. Law, who had both been listening to the women and observing the wedding ceremony on the dais. "Tell me, Louise," he went on, "wherever did those marvelous gold thrones come from? Are they from the Prominence?"

"They're from the grand ballroom."

"They're magnificent!"

"Quiet!" hissed an old crone on Dr. Law's left. "You're talking so much I can't hear what they're saying up there—"

"Madam," said Dr. Law loudly, "you couldn't hear them with a six-foot ear-trumpet—their voices aren't carrying back this far. If you weren't so deaf you would know that!"

Just then a loud cheer broke from the people up front—and then another cheer—and then a third: the nuptials had been performed! The ceremony was over! Miss Ester Hill was now Mrs. Conrad Venn!

The townspeople in the back took up the cheer: once—twice—thrice—

Ester was now smiling more broadly than ever, and slowly she began nodding at everyone, acknowledging their cheers: nodding first to the left and then gradually moving her head in an arc to the right, and then slowly back again . . .

At last Conrad raised both hands, signaling the mass of guests to be quiet.

"Ladies and gentlemen!" his voice boomed out. "You are invited, one and all, to descend to the grand ballroom and share in and witness the new-found happiness of the bride and bridegroom. The tables are laden. The wedding cake will be brought in shortly."

He paused as loud cheering greeted these words, and Ester smiled still more. From up front came many huzzas.

"Tables," he continued, "are also being set up on the grounds: on such a beautiful day, who would want to stay indoors and eat and drink when they can also go outdoors and eat and drink?"

The tower ballroom rang with laughter.

"And now—" Conrad stood up. He took Ester by both hands and helped her to rise from the deep seat of her throne, which was slightly lower than his. Mindful of her train, she turned to make sure it was all right. It had been draped over the right arm of the throne and then stretched out to the rear of the dais. Now several attendants hastened to straighten it for her. Sure that her train was all right, she smiled very happily and locked her arm in Conrad's.

For several seconds they stood there motionless, surveying the throng before them. There was a dead, respectful silence. Then Conrad passed his hand over the people, indicating a line between the dais and the door at the other end of the ballroom, and as Ester and he began descending the purple carpeted steps, a passageway slowly opened in the dense ranks of the guests.

"I have never seen him looking so well," whispered a handsome City lady after Conrad had passed by her.

"Or so happy," murmured her companion.

And farther along the passageway: "Doesn't he have a wonderful smile? When he smiles it seems to make everything perfect. I just have to smile back."

"Well," smiled a friend, "perhaps everything is perfect."

And still further along the passageway: "Do you suppose Conrad's in love?"

"I don't know."

"But doesn't he look as if he's in love?"

The ranks of townspeople stared at Conrad in awe and bewilderment. Even those who had seen him in formal dress on those Tuesday evenings when he used to dine at the Prominence Inn were overwhelmed as he passed close by them: so handsome, so rich-looking and regal, so sure of himself and his power. And how easily and comfortably all this sat upon him! Veritably, he seemed made for honors. All was his by nature, by right. The townspeople responded instinctively, scarcely breathing in his commanding presence.

The reception began in the grand ballroom, and for a full hour Conrad and Ester stood beneath the great glittering central chandelier receiving all of the guests, shaking their hands, smiling at them, and addressing a few words of greeting and welcome. Mr. and Mrs. Vale stood beside them and also greeted the guests; the Hills were far too busy with the actual management of the reception to act as hosts too. And the Vales, in a sense, represented the other wedding that had been performed. Despite the somber quality of that ceremony, the Vales were now their usual smiling and jovial selves. They joked with the guests about how plump they were and about how ladders had been necessary to get them onto the plateau . . .

"You should have seen how the servants had to push and pull me!" Mr. Vale laughed to Dr. Law. "I just hope I don't have to leave here in a hurry!"

"Yes, me too," agreed his wife.

Then Mr. Vale had an afterthought: "Of course, we could always jump!"

Dr. Law smiled at this, rather condescendingly, and moved on to shake hands with Conrad and Ester. Ester had been listening to the Vales and she said, very slowly: "I—couldn't—jump"—and her great double chins quivered with the effort—"someone—would have—to roll me off."

Dr. Law laughed. Ester's eyes, tiny now, almost hidden by puffs and rolls of flesh, twinkled at him for a moment, and then turned to Conrad. Lovingly she gazed at him, into his sharp black eyes.

"Don't worry, Ester," he smiled; "you'll never have to leave here. —Dr. Law"—Conrad extended his hand—"I am most happy to see you. Welcome to the Prominence."

"Congratulations, sir!" Dr. Law grasped Conrad's hand. "I am most happy to be here. And I wish you and your bride all the . . ."

Dr. Law's words were drowned by a great gasp from all the guests clustered near the main door of the ballroom. The gasp was one of surprise. It was quickly followed by a long, low *ahhhhh* of approval.

"The cake!" everyone exclaimed. "Look at the cake!"

The cake, borne on the shoulders of four stout men, was momentarily framed in the grand entrance.

"The cake! Make way for the cake!"

The wedding-cake procession slowly wound its way to the center of the ballroom. Two confectioners, making sure no one got under foot, led it. Harold brought up the rear. He was wearing a high chef's hat. He looked very tall. In his right hand he carried a broad ornamental sword.

Conrad smiled at Harold as the procession came to a halt before a long table covered with a white table-cloth and piled high with china dishes. Very carefully the bearers set down their burden on the end of the table and then withdrew while all the guests got as close as possible to have a better look at the cake.

It was a towering replica, in white and green and chocolate, of the Prominence set on the plateau. The steps leading up were etched in the side. The moat and water—made of clear icing— were there. The drawbridge was down, ready for crossing. There was all the landscaping, and the ivy on the walls. All the ramparts and battlements stood forth. The windows emitted a creamy light. And there on the top—on the very top turret— were two great figures standing hand in hand: striking reproductions of Conrad and Ester—he all in black and white, she all in white. Both were smiling.

Harold waited till everyone had got a good look at the cake, and the cries of astonishment and approval had quieted down somewhat. Then he stepped forward and touched the cake with the tip of the sword just to the left of the drawbridge—the plateau was one entire, very high layer. "The family sword is very dull," he whispered to Conrad, who smiled and nodded; Harold had revealed where the cake had already been cut. Conrad would only have to insert the blade and remove the slices. "With the compliments of the cook," Harold added, handing the sword to Conrad.

Harold watched while Conrad and Ester grasped the handle of the sword and detached the first slice of cake.

And he watched as Conrad impaled a piece of cake, loaded with green icing, on the end of a fork and held it out for Ester to eat.

And he watched anxiously as Conrad sampled a bite himself.

"It is very good, Harold," declared Conrad, savoring the morsel thoughtfully. "Yes, Harold, it is excellent cake."

Harold smiled gratefully, and left the ball room to return to his work in the great kitchen.

❦

The reception lasted the rest of the day and continued well into the night. Conrad and Ester mingled with all of the guests, talking to everyone and taking them around the Prominence and the grounds, until Ester got too tired and joined the Vales at the hosts' table on the south grounds.

Conrad even took several of his special friends into the great kitchen—Monte Springhorn and Rennie Bayard among others. And midst the general beehive of activity he singled out Harold and introduced him to those who hadn't met him before . . .

Mr. and Mrs. Vale, along with Ester, spent most of the afternoon and evening at the hosts' table, which was right at one corner of the drawbridge so that everyone crossing it for the first time—that is, the people from Cobb who couldn't come till late—could see where the hosts were and extend their best wishes. Ester didn't say very much, but she had a good time, and ate and drank along with everyone.

Mr. and Mrs. Vale obviously enjoyed being the hosts. They had nice words and smiles for all the townspeople, most of whom they knew by first name, and they never refused to drink with anyone who requested it. And when a place became empty at their table and someone new sat down, they would tell the waiter—when he brought food for the newcomer—to bring some for them too, because they knew no one liked to eat by himself. This they continued to do for upwards of eight hours, never flagging in good spirit or appetite, so that by the time the reception was about over all the members of the staff were talking about the amazing capacity of the Vales'. Word had even got back to Harold in the kitchen.

The morning following the reception Mr. and Mrs. Vale were found dead in bed . . . due to overindulgence, presumably.

VI

XXXIX

Within two months of the death of the Vales, their mansion was locked and boarded up. The entire contents of the house had been disposed of: some things were sold in Cobb, others were transported to the Prominence, and the remainder was auctioned off to bidders from the City. The administration of the rich Vale holdings fell to several of Mr. Vale's subordinates, hand-picked by Conrad.

By the end of the summer the Vale mansion and grounds were almost completely overrun by weeds and vines.

The Hill mansion fared much better. Mr. Hill retired formally from the mill. Mr. Renfrew took over and moved into the Hill mansion, by which time it too had been emptied of most of its contents. But the new occupants had, naturally, their own furnishings—plus a flock of young children—and promptly turned the deserted house back into a home, so that during the same time the Vale mansion was being reclaimed by nature, the old Hill mansion was being refurbished and made into a fitting and proper habitation for the administrator of the vast Hill holdings.

And so the year came to an end . . .

. . . Only by the remotest chance—from a City newspaper which found its way to Cobb in a crate of china for delivery to the Prominence—did the people of Cobb learn of the death and funeral of "Mrs. Harold Hill of the Prominence, Cobb," in the spring of the new year. The owner of the china shop could scarcely believe his eyes when he read the item, and he took the newspaper to his friend who ran the hardware store to confirm the wrinkled lines. Soon everyone in Cobb knew that poor Daphne had died of a "mysterious wasting disease" and had been buried beside her parents, Mr. and Mrs. Vale, in the Cobb family cemetery.

No one from Cobb had even been told!

Nor was this all the paper revealed: as it was passed from hand to hand in the assembled group in the tavern that night, someone started to read the front page instead of the back. And to the amazement of his listeners he read out a birth announcement: to Mr. and Mrs. Conrad Venn of the Prominence, Cobb, a son and heir. The naming ceremony would be held at the Prominence the evening of . . . A gala celebration would follow.

The group of listeners was dumbfounded: again, no one from Cobb had known a thing!

❧

The naming ceremony took place in the middle of April, evidently on the date announced. No one from Cobb was invited, but the demand for food deliveries to the Prominence suddenly sky-rocketed just as there was suddenly a great increase of visitors from the City. But none of these visitors spoke to any of the people of Cobb, and so no one could be sure they had come especially for the naming ceremony and for the celebration to follow. However, it was noted that all of these visitors were dressed as if for a great occasion. To be sure, the visitors to the Prominence always dressed very grandly . . .

On the evening of the day set for the naming, the people of Cobb looked at the Prominence with awe: it was lit up as they had never seen it lit up before. From every window of the enormous Gothic structure, light streamed out—it seemed as if every light and every chandelier and every light in every chandelier were turned on, pouring forth its brightest radiance, so that, seen from Cobb, the Prominence loomed out in the night like a diamond of glacial proportions with millions of facets all glittering and glowing. People gathered in the streets to stare at it, and talk among themselves.

Children said it looked like a great big star all on fire . . .

The following evening the Prominence was lit up just as much, as if the celebration were still going on.

And the following evening . . .

And the next . . . and the next . . . and the next . . .

And the next . . .

Epilogue

Anyone traveling on the road from the City to Cobb, whether in the evening or late at night or in the early hours of the morning, saw lights blazing from dozens of windows in the castle-like structure high up on the plateau. No noise drifted across the trees and down to the road; the distance was too great. Yet, if the traveler was returning from his stay at the Prominence, he knew there was great life and activity and gayety within those thick stone walls. Twenty-four hours a day revelry prevailed. There was feasting and drinking and dancing. Music was played at all hours. The huge central ballroom was filled with talking and laughing and frolicking people. The great dining table was heaped with all conceivable kinds of food.

Servants poured from endless bottles of wine. In the two other ballrooms the same scene was repeated on a smaller scale.

And were the traveler granted entrance to the Prominence kitchen, he would see amazing white-clothed figures running around, like ants, among the enormous stoves and steaming tables. He could scarcely distinguish one figure from another, yet he'd know they must come and go in shifts because at no time in the day was there any lessening of their number: the ovens never cooled, the burners were never shut off, the tables never stopped steaming, the sinks were never empty. Pots and pans were cleaned and put away while others were being taken out and used, and still others were brought back from the different dining rooms to be cleaned and started on their cycle again. Trays of dirty dishes and glasses were continually brought to the kitchen, and other trays laden with food were just as continually leaving. In other parts of the great kitchen white figures sat hunched over piles of vegetables—cleaning, cutting, scraping and paring; here and there were large worktables, where similar-looking figures labored over multitudinous cuts and kinds of meats; in between were smaller working areas, where more esoteric preparations of food were being performed. And while all this was going on, the doors at the rear of the kitchen kept admitting people with fresh supplies of everything: meat, game, fowl, fish, cheese, vegetables, etc.—some of the things to be put to immediate use in the kitchen, others to be stored in the coolers or the pantries.

In the center of the great kitchen there was a single, very high stool. On this stool perched a thin figure in a tall chef's hat fourteen hours a day. He was relieved by a smaller, rotund man, also dressed all in white, and with a slightly shorter chef's hat. Both of them always had, either in their hand or resting across their lap, a great long wooden spoon. With this they attracted attention to their words, corrected erring cooks and tasted food. They oversaw everything; they were responsible for what left the kitchen. Their word was law, and of the two, the one who sat perched on the stool fourteen hours of the day was in charge: the rotund man worked the floor the four hours when he wasn't on the stool.

Several times a day one or two of the cooks ran up to the man on the stool and whispered in his ear, then a few minutes later the large double doors of the kitchen were thrown open and two huge valets in livery appeared, supporting by both his arms a fantastically fat figure in expensive and bedizened evening clothes. Slowly the three of them would make their way to the stool. Everything would suddenly become quiet in the kitchen, though the same work proceeded apace—perhaps a little faster than before. As soon as the great figure appeared, the man on the stool would turn to him, and when the figure came up to the stool the chef would bend down to hear what he had to say. Sometimes he would nod at the words and smile. Other times he would dart a furious glance in the direction of someone in the kitchen. When the man on the stool was the short rotund one, the conversation never lasted more than a minute or two. But when the chef was there, the talk sometimes lasted fifteen minutes or more, and often before the enormous figure turned to leave, assisted by the two valets, he would pat the leg of the cook with unmistakable affection. Then, when he had made his way slowly out of the kitchen, his words of praise or criticism were transmitted to the individuals meriting them.

And many other times during the day one of the dining-room servants came into the kitchen and whispered to the chef or his assistant that the house steward was coming, and then a middle-aged man of just above average height, rather thin, in an ornate uniform—black with gold buttons—appeared. For a moment he would just stand in the doorway, surveying everything. Then he would go up to the stool and give some instruction to the cook in charge: to have a special dish prepared, correct something, alter the menu, etc.—on orders from . . . The house steward resembled the chef both in build and face. Every member of the Prominence staff was terrified of him except the chef and the housekeeper. These three had a special relationship, though this was open and obvious only in the case of the chef and the house-keeper, who was in charge of all the maids and cleaners, and responsible for the maintenance of and supplies for all the living quarters and guest rooms in the Prominence. The housekeeper was a middle-aged woman, rather thin and extremely energetic. She worked more than sixteen hours a day, and the maids carry-ing out her orders could never foretell when she might suddenly appear in some remote wing of the Prominence to watch them at their tasks or inspect the work they had already done. This was quite a job, since in addition to the permanent residents there were sometimes as many as two hundred guests at the Prominence. The housekeeper was also responsible, along with the house steward, for keeping all of the accounts at the Prom-inence.

Three or four times a day, while the chef was working, the housekeeper came into the kitchen to relax for a few minutes from her work. She would go up to the high stool; sometimes the cook leaned down, and she would stretch up and kiss him lightly on the cheek. While she whispered to him he would signal to one of the soup cooks, and a bowl of light broth was brought over and handed to the housekeeper. Sometimes she requested a stool, and then one of the pantry boys would run and bring her a short stool; she would sit down and lean against one of the cupboards and drink her broth and watch the chef at his job. As she watched him and sipped her broth, gradually relaxing, a contented and happy smile would light up her coun-tenance . . .

Besides some permanent house guests—permanent in the sense that few members of the staff could remember when they weren't there—the only other frequent visitor to the great kitchen was an enormous fat woman. She too needed the assistance of valets for the activity of walking. Indeed, it was a frequent observation of these valets that the day was fast approaching when she would be too fat to walk and would have to be moved about from place to place in a sort of sedan chair. The valets were dreading this day because, as they said, so long as she still made the effort to walk she eschewed the climbing of steps; but when her walking days were over she would probably want them to carry her up and down all kinds of stairs.

Her arrival in the kitchen was heralded by no one. She simply appeared in the great doorway and then slowly made her way, assisted by the valets, to the high stool. The chef—she only came when he was there—would bend down and pat her affectionately on her huge arm, and call to one of the confectioners to bring her a little something he was making. She munched the goody and listened—apparently—to whatever the chef had to say. She herself rarely said anything. After several minutes she would signal to the valets that she was ready to leave. The cook would pat her on the arm again, smile a little as a slightly—and unexpected—dreamy look would momentarily appear in his eyes, and then he would call to the confectioner again, who came running over with another sample of his work. One final pat by the cook, and then the huge woman would start to make her way slowly toward the great double doors . . .

❧

Life at the Prominence was one unending feast.

The shopkeepers of Cobb were hard-pressed to keep up with the fantastic demands for deliveries of food. Of course, they were gradually becoming wealthy on the business, so they did their best to supply the Prominence with all of its needs. The same was true of the fishermen and hunters: at any hour of the day or night they could be seen on the Vale lakes and on the Hill lands. So long as the supply of fish and game lasted they were assured of a good income. Their only worry was that the demands of the Prominence were too great for nature to supply—that one day the lakes would cease to yield fish and the lands would cease to breed game. Then what would become of them . . . ?

❧

. . . Another year goes by and the pace of consumption at the Prominence seems actually to have increased. Eating there literally goes on endlessly . . .

. . . And the rumors in town!

That: fantastically outlandish and expensive concoctions are prepared there.

That: the two estates are being bankrupted to pay for the endless series of gigantic feasts.

That: four servants are kept just to help Mr. Venn up and down from his chair.

That: Mrs. Venn is so fat she can't bend her arms to feed herself and people have to do it for her—pushing the food into her mouth—and six servants are required to carry her sedan chair up and down stairs.

That: vomitoriums have been installed in the central ballroom.

. . . And all sorts of unbelievable tales . . .

Harry Kressing is a pseudonym.

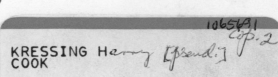